HELIGAN
Lost Gardens, [

Written and compiled by Candy Smit
Running text © Candy Smit
Designed by Charlie Webster
Printed by Francis Antony, St Austell
on paper sourced from well managed forests, with ECF low chlorine content

Published by Heligan Gardens Ltd; 2008,
to mark the 90th Anniversary of the Armistice
Second edition 2010
Updated and reprinted 2012
ISBN 978-1-900270-02-1

For further information on the history of Heligan see the book
The Lost Gardens of Heligan by Tim Smit and DVDs of 1997 & 1999 Channel 4
TV series – and on Heligan's historic plantings, see the books *Heligan Survivors*,
The Heligan Vegetable Bible and *Heligan: Fruit, Flowers and Herbs* by Philip McMillan Browse

The gardens are open daily all year round
(excepting Christmas Eve and Christmas Day)

The Lost Gardens of Heligan, Pentewan, St Austell, Cornwall PL26 6EN

Telephone: 01726 845100

www.heligan.com

CONTENTS

Interior of the ruined Head Gardener's Office, 1991

FOREWORD

I first adventured into the grounds at Heligan with Tim in the early spring of 1990, only weeks after the Great Storm had devastated the South West. A master of words and inspiration but initially with barely a connection in horticulture, Tim soon innocently spun the name "The Lost Gardens" as an evocative promotional tool for his fantastic obsession. But I myself can vouch that this was – and still is – no glib catch-phrase; it was rooted in the fascinating, brooding reality that we experienced on numerous early forays and which somehow remains.

Tim was hooked on Heligan from Day One. He was fired to unravel the human story of what had gone on before, what it had once been and why it had crumbled into such haunting devastation. With his early partner, John Nelson, he discovered personal artefacts, as it were, left at the scene of some silent catastrophe; rusting scissors on a rotting shelf in the collapsing vinery, an enormous kettle amongst ferns in the hearth of a shadowy roofless building and a small zinc bucketful of coal, deserted at the top of a flight of steps to an old boiler, all silted up...

Tim's curiosity, drive and ability to be all things to all people (as well as his inability to accept the answer "No" to anything!) drew together an unregulated band of enthusiasts and specialists from many walks of life, who achieved in but a few years (to quote *The Times*) "...the garden restoration of the century." I, meanwhile, had only peripheral involvement at that time; diary, address book, correspondence, wondering how to pay the next bill – and along the way, making new friends, learning the exotic names of plants I'd never seen before and making occasional trips to the latest 'frontier'. I slowly got a feel for it all. As the clearance proceeded and treasures continued to emerge, we became aware that the very ground itself spoke of tragic loss; caution and respect were the silent order of every waking hour, every conversation, every sweep of the scythe or footstep into the unknown.

One day John and Tim were making slow progress through a thicket of bamboo outside a large brick gateway into a walled garden. There was a sense they were homing in on the heart of Heligan. They carved their way through bramble meshed above head-height, wrapped around substantial self-set trees and shrouding the skeletons of frames near a range of derelict buildings. Hours later and but yards further on, in a two-storey building that was little more than a pile of rubble at the far corner,

Derelict Paxton House, 1991

3

Collapsed Carnation (Orchid?) House in the Flower Garden, 1991

they 'struck gold'. What they then discovered in a moment of memorable exhilaration were those signatures in the Thunderbox Room above a date, August 1914. At once they recognised that these provided the rationale for the whole restoration project that ensued. Here, in the old garden toilet, the working men had left their marks before Heligan fell into its long, gentle slumber. The story for some, as it all unravelled, was heart-breakingly sad.

Today "The Lost Gardens of Heligan" is a living memorial to these staff and many more from Heligan's past, some of whom gave their lives for their country. It is still all deliberately 'labour intensive'. We have undertaken not only a structural restoration but a return to past practice, embraced by the workplace of our forefathers. There is a tangible sense we can still learn from them, though little was ever recorded.

The Lost Gardens are also a haven for our visitors from the pressures of twenty-first century life. They too realise there is something of significance here. We walk into the past, brought alive before us, not in some contrived fashion but with unbelievable ease. We realise that, while the outside world has undoubtedly changed over the past century, the patterns in human relations endure... all the passions, the frailties and accidents of fate. Heligan is, and always has been, not just a garden full of plants with amazing stories to be told, but of people too; all part of life's rich tapestry woven between themselves in the context of the wider world – whatever the era. If it is hard even to describe, understand, predict or control what goes on amongst us now, how can we expect ever to be able to neatly package the past?

Notwithstanding the current separation of the Gardens from Heligan House (to which there is no public access), there is still much visitor interest in the history of Heligan – both in the Tremayne family who occupied the "Mansion" for over three centuries and in the horticultural triumphs achieved by four past generations. There is some accessible Heligan archive in both the Cornwall and North Devon Record Offices, but much was lost in a fire in 1949. I myself am ill-equipped to compile a comprehensive record.

However, many of us are in a position to trace our own family histories with comparative ease back over a hundred years and most are at least aware of the woes of our forefathers through two world wars. We share a sense of losing something precious that preceded their demise and we feel somehow that this history still has relevance to our lives today; though it is almost out of reach, as barely any now remain to tell the tales. Not so long ago I constructed my own family tree back five generations on a single large sheet, brought to life with old photographs, and I know that my grandfather was not alone in losing three brothers to these tragic causes. I can identify immediately with the sort of issues that constrain freely given information, even after decades.

As a result, respectful of personal privacy, we have not been particularly proactive in pursuing the human history of Heligan; but have elected to wait on fate to filter it through. We are a part of this place now and tend and cherish it as others have done before us. We have to live with the consequences of our actions – so 'do as we would be done by'. Our ethos is to be non-intrusive, to let the past find its own place, its own freedom almost to discover itself. I believe many of our visitors subconsciously connect with Heligan on this basis and return endlessly to somewhere which offers solace and demands nothing of them, yet 'means something'. They can absorb as much as they wish. Maybe through touching on the

Entrance to the Head Gardener's Office, 1991

The old Tool Shed in the Melon Yard, 1991

fragments of others' lives we are better equipped to understand and live our own.

I have been in a position to receive and save anecdotes as and when they have been offered and it has been a real privilege for me and my colleagues to meet some of the descendants of past players, both 'upstairs' and 'downstairs' at Heligan over the last century or more. The following pages constitute little more than a collage of pictures, cuttings and reminiscences, illustrating a dramatic century of life at Heligan since its glorious, late Victorian heyday until its absolute moment of demise. In its insignificant totality, however, I hope this booklet not only manages to give a flavour of past achievements and lifestyle and the exceptional sacrifice of earlier generations; but also a sense that every one of us now, whatever our lot in life, can make a contribution towards establishing a productive balance with nature in the future, as well as peace in our time.

I am very grateful for the years of friendship and generosity from the contemporary descendants of the Tremayne Family – Damaris Tremayne, Penelope, Antonia and John Willis. Furthermore I am honoured to have shared with local families memories of gardeners and the gardens past. I am respectful of the desire of Gill and Sue *née* Thomas to tell the story of their own family at Heligan in years to come. The extraordinary photographs above and at the end of the book were taken by Herbie Knott more than a year after the Gardens were rediscovered. I can but leave these images to speak for themselves.

Candy Smit
Heligan, July 2008

Opposite *Fading signatures on the lime plaster of the Thunderbox Room*

John Claude Lewis Tremayne was born in 1869, the youngest of the five children of John Tremayne and his wife, Mary. His only brother, Perys Edmund, died when he was a baby, so it was John Claude Lewis, aka "Jack", who succeeded his father as Squire of Heligan. At this point, in 1901, his mother was still alive and he was already married to Eleanor Elizabeth Rashleigh; but before long he was head of the household on his own. Jack's father John was one of three preceding generations who developed the House and Gardens at Heligan and it was during his fifty-year stewardship that the reputation of both – and the family's position at the heart of the community – reached its climax. Jack, meanwhile, was endowed with considerable artistry, which he devoted to design and ornamentation of both House and Gardens and to his not inconsiderable achievements in recording both with his camera.

Captain J. C. L. Tremayne in the uniform of the Duke of Cornwall's Light Infantry

Sampson Tremayne's arrival here in the mid-sixteenth century brought the Tremaynes to Heligan. During the following two centuries developments were focused on reconstructing and expanding "Heligan Barton" and on the creation of the Gardens and buildings immediately surrounding it. In 1766 Henry Hawkins Tremayne unexpectedly inherited Heligan on the death of his brother Lewis and it was his strength of character, wise marriage, good fortune and long life that secured a transformation of not only the whole Heligan Estate but also the family inheritance.

Squire Henry Hawkins can be considered the founder of the Gardens as we know them today, installing shelterbelts

The crest of the Tremayne family incorporating 'trois mains'

In the 1890s Heligan House was surrounded by immaculate formal gardens

and rides around the whole estate and separating what we now know as the Northern Gardens from the surrounding farmland. He installed the infrastructure necessary both for future technical developments in productive gardening (which included the magnificent walled garden), and for the creation of the Pleasure Grounds. The following three squires, somewhat unhelpfully all christened "John", were largely responsible for the introduction of plants from all over the world.

As an MP, John Hearle spent much time in London; he is likely to have been an early member of the Horticultural Society of London and would have picked up on new trends. He was passionate not only about his farm but also about the woods back at Heligan. He was responsible for the earliest introductions of many coniferous trees, as well as the first camellias. Through his marriage he became connected to the Lemon family locally, who had plant hunting connections and received seed via Kew, almost direct on arrival.

Hence Heligan's fine collection of rhododendrons – an enthusiasm inherited by John Hearle's son, John, who became Squire in 1851, at the peak of Sir Joseph Hooker's plant hunting expeditions. Though not gifted with good health, John's passion for new plants later extended to the science of hybridisation and to encouraging his son (Jack) to continue to develop the Gardens. The latter years of the nineteenth century saw them introduce numerous species, from as far away as Japan and South America, and the wondrous creation of what we now call "The Jungle" – Jack's inspired, exotic essay in textural foliage, written upon the Cornish landscape.

Family Tree of the Tremaynes
THE SQUIRES WHO CREATED THE GARDENS

b.1709 d.1756 John TREMAYNE m. Grace HAWKINS b.1708 d.1765
1735

Lewis
b.1739
d.1766
buried St Ewe

Henry Hawkins m. **Harriet**
b.1741 (Heligan) 1767 HEARLE
· ordained 1766 b.
Squire 1766 d.1805
· Mayor of Penryn
· Chaplain Bodmin Assizes
· Vice President Cornwall
  Agricultural Society
d. 1829
buried St Ewe

Grace m. Charles
b.1744 RASHLEIGH
m.1776
d.1820

John Hearle m. Caroline Matilda LEMON
(only child) b.1780 1813 b.
· MP Cwll 1806-25 (London) d.1864 (London)
Squire 1829
· High Sheriff 1831
· Vice President R.H.S. of
  Cornwall from inception 1833
d.1851 (Dawlish)

John m. Mary Charlotte Martha
1860 CRESPIGNY
b.
(oldest surviving son b.15-4-1825 d.1917
of 7 children all Squire 1851 (eldest daughter of
born in London) · High Sheriff 1859 Baron VIVIAN)
· MP 1874-80 & 1884-85
d.1901 Biarritz
buried St Ewe 15-4-1901

Grace Damaris Matilda m. Charles Hagart
b.1864 1889 BABINGTON
Croan transferred 1914
d.

John Claude Lewis
b.1869 (Youngest of 5 children,
  all born in London)
· Captain in D.C.L.I.
m. Eleanor Elizabeth RASHLEIGH
  1897-1903 (dissolved)
Squire 1901
d.1949 (Italy)
· buried St Ewe

John Tremayne m. Cecily
b.1891 1916 BERESFORD HOPE
(second of 5 sons - all b.1894
served in the Great War) d.1953
· Lt. Col. Royal Flying Corps
· Legion of Honour, D.S.O.
· Croix de Guerre
· Retired in rank of
  Air Vice Marshal
d.1979

Damaris Jean
b.1918-2010

Penelope m. Harold Anthony WILLIS
b.1921 1960 b.1924 d.2008

Antonia Mary Damaris
b.1961

John Richard Tremayne
b.1962 m.1986 Katharine White

THE WEST BRITON – August 5, 1886

BAZAAR AT HELIGAN

In aid of the funds of Mevagissey Church, a bazaar was opened in the grounds of Heligan, St Austell, the residence of Mr John Tremayne. For many years Mevagissey Church has been in a very dilapidated state, but simultaneously with the appointment of the Rev. E. M. Perry, as curate-in-charge, a movement was initiated for its restoration, in which Mr. Tremayne evinced the warmest interest. Plans having been prepared by Mr. Piers St. Aubyn, the contract was let to Mr. Kitto, of Mevagissey, and the work is proceeding. The church has to be almost entirely re-built, only the walls being left standing, and at present service is being held in the school-room. The total cost of the restoration is expected to be about £2,000, besides special gifts, such as the east window, which is to be the gift of Lady Vivian in memory of Lord Vivian. Of the sum needed about £1,000 had been promised up to the opening of the bazaar on Monday.

There is a lovely spot in the grounds of Heligan, which is now called Flora's Green, but which is said to have been anciently the bowling green of the establishment. It is now a most beautiful piece of greensward surrounded by trees and rhododendrons, and at the sides of it the bazaar stalls were located. Their pretty ornamentation, the flags and streamers which spread across the green, the dresses of the ladies, and the uniforms of the bandsmen enclosed in this fair ring, made a pretty sight. Of all the stalls the most interesting and attractive was the first one on the right of the entrance, outside of which swung the sign of "The Jersey Cow." It was a sign painted from life with much more artistic truth than is usually displayed for such purposes, and it bore the signature of "G. Tremayne, 1886." The stall was divided into two parts, and over the top of it ran the enticing announcement, "The Land Floweth with Milk and Honey," and the didactic motto, "The hand of the industrious maketh riches." Inside were fair dairy-maids and waitresses dispensing good things– Miss Maud Tremayne, Miss Jones Loyd, Mrs Lucas, and Mrs Holland. Across the green were the work stalls laden with articles of artistic construction, or calculated to be of useful service. The first stall was held

Mr. John Tremayne

Hon. Mrs. Tremayne

by the Hon. Mrs. Tremayne, the Misses Tremayne, and the Misses Jones Loyd (of Langleybury, Hertfordshire) ; the second by Lady Williams (for Mrs. Williams, of Caerhays Castle), and Mrs Kyndon ; the third by Miss Ball, assisted by Miss Sowell ; the fourth by Miss Smith, assisted by Miss Bessie Smith, of Ventonwyn ; the fifth, by Mrs. Jago and Miss Jago ; and the sixth by Mrs. Perry. Mr. Tremayne and Mr. Webber were unremitting in their attentions to the visitors to a museum of real curiosities, many of them from foreign lands ; and in a tent in an adjoining field Professor Herman Robel, of Truro, delighted periodical audiences with some wonderful conjuring performances. Some of his tricks were novel, and all were very clever. Mr. Kinsman, of St. Austell, created great astonishment and no little amusement by his exhibitions of a galvanic battery.

Besides the Rev. E. M. Perry and Mr. Gillard, whose services were rendered wherever they were required, and Mr. Perry, of Stonehouse, who kindly attended to superintend the construction and arrangement of the stalls, the following gentlemen lent their aid as members of committees : —For Finance—Messrs. H. Rowe (chairman), J. Kitto, G. C. Pedlar, J. Kendall, R. Johns, E. Burnett, R. Nicholls, J. Farrar, J. Law, R. Teague, F. R. Hicks, and J. Warren. Amusements—Messrs. White (piano), Capt. Bale, C. Hicks, F. Kendall, W. Bovey, T. Cloake, and S. Chesterfield. Refreshments—Messrs. J. Michell, W. Kendall, R. Michell, S. Gillard, R. Julyan, T. Hicks, R. Clark, J. Wills, J. T. Rowe, J. Venning, J. Warne, W. Lawry, J. Lanyon, W. Furse, Capt. Farran, F. Stocker, T. Mellow, S. Over, and H. Lobb. Mr. P. C. Bovell, assisted by Mr. R. S. Rowe acted as secretary. There were a luncheon and tea, the following doing duty at the latter :—Mrs. Warren, Mrs Nicholls, Mrs Teague, Mrs. Holland, Mrs. Kelly, Mrs. Lugg, Mrs. Clarke, and the Misses Mitchell, Hicks, Mellow, Edwards, Retallack, Farren, Body, Tollerbey, Puckey, Johns, Hunkin, Baron, Harris, and Smith. The band stand was occupied by the St. Austell Volunteer Band, who played an excellent programme of music, under the direction of Mr. Jago.

Considering the many counter attractions of Bank Holiday, the attendance was very good. Mr. and Mrs. Tremayne had several guests, including Col. and Lady Elizabeth Byng, Mr. and Mrs. Lucas, Major and Mrs. Roebuck, Mr. C. Grylls, and Mr. Rawlinson, D.C.L.I., and among other visitors were Sir Vyell Vyvyan, Bart., Mr. Francis Glanville, Lady Sawle and Miss Sawle, Mr. Edmond Carlyon, and the Rev. A. Lawerence. The Bazaar was continued on Tuesday.

THE ST. AUSTELL STAR – Friday August 8, 1890

COMING OF AGE FESTIVITIES AT HELIGAN.

PRESENTATION TO MR. JOHN C. L. TREMAYNE.

Friday was the twenty-first birthday of Mr. Claude Lewis, the only son of Mr. Tremayne of Heligan, near St. Austell ; and the event was celebrated by a presentation to him on behalf of the tenants, agents, and stewards, and workmen on the estate. A large tent was erected for the purpose by the Cornish Tent Company, Tywardreath, and about three hundred tenants and visitors were entertained at luncheon and tea (capitally supplied by Mr. McTurk, of St. Austell). The excellent band of the St. Austell Volunteers, under Mr. Jago, also added much to the day's enjoyment. The presentation consisted of four magnificent entrée dishes, and was organised by a committee, of which Mr. T. Hicks was chairman, Mr. J. C. Lawry treasurer, and Mr. C. G. Pedlar secretary. The presentation was made at the luncheon, at which Mr. Tremayne presided, and there were also present the Honble. Mrs. Tremayne, Mr. John C. L. Tremayne, Lady Vivian, Miss Maud Tremayne, Mrs. Babington, Mr. and Mrs. H. H. Tremayne, and Miss Tremayne, of Plymouth ; Mr. G. R. G. Carlyon, of Tregrehan ; Mr. Hugh Neville, of Butleigh ; Mr. Hender Molesworth St. Aubyn, of Clowance ; Mr. and Mrs. William Coode, Mr. H. Whitford and Miss Whitford, of St. Columb ; Rev. Nigel and Mrs. Neville, of St. Ewe ; Rev. E. M. Perry, of Mevagissey ; Mrs. Veale and Mr. J. E. Veale, Mr. and Mrs. Tresawna, and Mr. and Mrs. W. Trethewey, Probus ; the Misses Grant, Mrs. Gearing, Mr. and Mrs. Lukes.

After "The Queen" the presentation was made by Mr. J. C. Lawry, in the place of Mr. R. Julyan, the

oldest tenant in direct line, who was prevented from attending by family bereavement.

Mr. JOHN C. L. TREMAYNE in reply, said : Ladies and gentlemen, I have never before attempted to make a speech in public and I am afraid I shall make rather a failure of it. However, I hope you will forgive me, and will think as well of me as you can. (Applause.) The present occasion is particularly difficult, because I cannot find words to express to you my thanks, first, for coming here, and, secondly, for the beautiful gift you have made me in these four dishes. As long as I live I shall look upon them as the most valuable things I have, and I hope they will ever remind me—as I am sure they will—of your extreme kindness to me, and will help me to be half as good a man as my father. (Applause.) I am quite aware that it is not through any merit of my own that these dishes are given me, but through the goodness of my father and mother ; and I can only add that I hope that I shall always be a help to my father, and that I shall have the honour of knowing you all better one day. (Applause.) I again thank you one and all for your great kindness in coming here today. I hope it will not be the last time by many we shall meet, and I wish you all the best of health and happiness. (Loud applause.)

Mr. R.S. Olver gave "the health of Mr. and the Hon. Mrs. Tremayne and family."

Mr. T. STOCKER said he had very great pleasure in supporting this toast. He had not been a troublesome tenant, for he had not usually seen Mr. Gillard more than once a year—(a laugh)—but he had met with little acts of kindness at his hands and the hands of Mr. Tremayne. As an instance of this, Mr. Stocker mentioned his having received willing permission to take Mr. Spurgeon's orphan boys over Heligan, and those orphan boys from London did not at all object to the Cornish cream from the Jerseys with which Mr. Gillard feasted them. That was illustrative of the kindly feeling of the family at Heligan, and the whole neighbourhood would wish him to express to them the heartiest good wishes for their welfare. (Applause.)

Mr. TREMAYNE, in reply said : Ladies and gentleman, kind friends and neighbours. I thank you most sincerely for coming here to-day. It is not an easy task for me to speak under these circumstances, being, as I am, under the influence of very strong emotion. (Applause). It is an event of no inconsiderable importance to me that my only son has to-day reached manhood. (Applause). I thank you very much for your reception of him to-day, and join my thanks to those which he has expressed, in my opinion, in a very creditable manner for a beginner—(applause)—for the exceedingly generous and liberal presents made to him. I see four most beautiful dishes contributed by the

Mr. John C. L. Tremayne

tenants, old servants and workmen upon these Cornish estates ; and on one side I see an exceedingly handsome piece of plate given by the tenants at Sydenham, and on the other side a similar offering from the tenants on the North Devon estates. I hope that whenever my son looks upon these he will remember they are the evidences of the kindest and the most affectionate feeling towards his father and mother, and I hope they will remind him of duties which before long he will have to undertake and the responsibility which will in the natural course of events devolve upon him (Applause). I have to thank you, not only for the kind way in which you have spoken of myself and of Mrs. Tremayne, but also of all the members of my family. From the first day that Mrs. Tremayne left her Cornish home to come here and found another Cornish home, now nearly thirty years ago, I know it has been the aim and object of her life to fulfil the duties she was called upon to perform with reference to every tenant, or dependant, or workman on the estate or friend of the family. (Applause). I know it has been the aim and object of her life to bring up her children to love their Cornish home—(applause)—and respect their Cornish neighbours, and to take their position in Cornish society. (Applause). Mr. Olver has been kind enough to say that as a landlord I have tried to perform my duty. (Applause). I can assure you that upon every occasion when I have had business to transact with my tenants, I have endeavoured honestly and fairly to do my duty. (Applause). And if I have succeeded in that, it is because we have always proceeded upon the old and the Christian principle of forbearance one towards the other ;

we have recognised the true socialistic doctrine that we must act in co-operation, and in cordial union one with the other—that the landlord and tenants are partners in the same concern—that when times are prosperous and there is a smile on the tenants faces, that smile is reflected on the landlord's face, and that when times are distressful and difficult, those troubles show a reflection upon the landlord's face, and was an occasion upon which the help and assistance of the landlord is demanded, and in my case I hope that assistance has never been withheld. (Applause). I have said that I am speaking under feelings of very strong emotion, and you can easily understand why. I see before me men whom I have known as tenants of my estates as long as I have been the possessor of them. I see the sons and grandsons of men whom I remember as tenants of these estates, and I hope and pray most devoutly that in the same way—although there must in the natural course of events be changes—that my son may live to see the estates handed down from those who now occupy those estates to sons yet to come and succeed them. (Applause). But it is not only by reason of having a good tenantry, as I have, that a landlord obtains a good name. He is dependant in a very great degree upon his agents and stewards. (Applause). Now, I have been blessed in that respect in a most remarkable degree, and it is altogether beyond my power to adequately convey to my agents and stewards my extraordinary sense of the very great debt of gratitude I owe to them. In Mr. W. Coode, the son of a man who was my agent before ; in Mr. Whitford, the son of a man who was my agent before ; in Mr. Gillard—(loud applause) – who, before commencing his long and valuable services here, was a tenant upon my Devonshire estate ; and in my dear friend Mr. Smale, also the son of a man who was my steward before him, I assert that I have a body of agents and stewards, not inferior in the highest qualifications of mankind to anyone in the world. (Applause). Although they might be employed by the landlord, they were all interested in exercising and seeing that the landlord exercised the strictest measure of justice to the tenants. (Applause). I cannot conclude without alluding also to the workmen present. Many of them are the sons and grandsons of men whom I remember working on this estate when I was a boy. Many of them are now of course up in years and grey of head, whom I remember strong, and lusty, and cheery boys. So time goes on, and if I have done my duty to these men in any way which entitles me to their respect, I desire no greater praise than their commendation. (Applause). I drink to the health of the tenants, agents, and stewards, and workmen of my Heligan and Croan Estates, and may the blessing of God rest upon you all. (Loud applause.)

Mr. T. Hicks, Peruppa, Mr. W. Coode, Mr. Gillard, and Mr. J. Wonnacott responded. Afterwards the visitors rambled over the beautiful grounds, and there was dancing on the green. Tea was held in the tent at 6.30 and all the proceedings passed off most happily.

The 1890s

In September 1894 the Hon. Mrs. Tremayne opened the Grand Indian Palace Bazaar in the Market Hall, St Austell, featuring electric lighting, heating and fountains. In 1896 the local fishing village of Mevagissey was one of the first in the country to have electric street lighting installed. Incidentally, 1896 also witnessed the first Olympic Games of the modern era, held in Athens, prompted by the efforts of Pierre Coubertin, a contemporary of Jack Tremayne. Meanwhile, the same year Harry Williams would have been at Heligan; a garden then at the peak of its reputation, employing a career-oriented foreman gardener (as outlined below).

THE WEST BRITON – February 1951

80th BIRTHDAY

Grand Old Man of Cornish Gardening

The "Grand Old Man" of Cornish horticulture, Mr. Harry Williams, of Treva, 18 Adelaide-road, Redruth, who is widely recognised to be an authority on the subject, has received many congratulations on the celebration of his 80th birthday, on Tuesday. Mr. Williams, who enjoys good health, is a familiar and greatly-respected figure in the town, in whose general welfare he continues to take a deep and active interest.

Born at Tolgus, Redruth, Mr. Williams, who throughout his life has been a keen student and a prolific reader of good literature, attended the old Redruth Wesleyan Day School, whose headmaster was a celebrated local educationist, Thomas Collins. Mr. Williams commenced his life-long association with the soil and with horticultural products by serving a five years' apprenticeship in the beautiful gardens of Tolvean, for long the home of the Lanyon family. Subsequently he went as an improver to join the staff in the gardens at Trevarno, Sithney, then the residence of Mr. W. N. Bickford-Smith, for some time M.P. for the old Truro-Helston Division. In 1893 he left to become a student gardener at the Royal Botanical Gardens, Kew, where he studied for three years. His first appointment after leaving Kew was as foreman at Heligan, the Cornish residence of Mr. John W. (?) Tremayne, whose garden was famous for its unique collection of trees and shrubs. A year later Mr. Williams became head gardener to Mr. E. B. Beauchamp, at Trevince, Gwennap. His final position was that of head gardener at Tolvean, Redruth, then the home of Mr. Alfred Lanyon, where he remained for 40 years up to the time of his retirement, and served under three generations of the Lanyon family. During Mr. Williams' long term of service there the gardens became famous for their outstanding collections of shrubs and flowers, and were visited by gardeners and horticulturists from a wide area. For many years one of the most popular features of the magnificent horticultural tent at Redruth Exhibition Society's annual shows was the lovely assortment of shrubs, plants, and flowers from the gardens, staged by Mr. Williams.

HELIGAN, CORNWALL.

The history of the Tremaynes, of Tremayne, forms no inconsiderable portion in the long and interesting annals of the county of Cornwall ; few families have more worthily maintained the leading position which they have held in the westernmost county from time almost immemorial.

The manor of Tremayne, situate in the parish of St. Martins-in-Meneage, on the banks of Helford-Haven, is said to have given name and origin to the ancestors of Perys or Peres Tremayne, who resided there, temp. Edward III. John Tremayne, of this family, who was sheriff in 1486-87, had a brother called Richard, who resided at Trogonan, and who is thus noticed by Carew : "At the adjoyning Saint Tue (St. Ewe) dwelleth master Richard Tremayne, descended from a younger brother, of Calocumbhouse in Devon, who being learned in the lawes, is yet to learne, or a least to practise, how to make other proffit thereby, then by hoording up treasure of gratitude, in the mindsfull breasts of poore and rich, on whom he, gratis, bestoweth the fruites of his paines and knowledge." Another distinguished member of the family, Lewis Tremayne, commanded a regiment of foot for Charles I., and was Lieutenant–Governor of Pendennis Castle.

The manor of Heligan was, at an early period, the property of the Heligans, from whom it passed by female heirs to the Tregarthians and Whitleighs; and from the latter by co-heiresses to the families of Grenville and Hals. One of the Tremaynes purchased the property at a very early date, probably during the earlier years of the sixteenth century. William Tremayne began to build Heligan in 1597, and first inhabited the house in 1604. Sir John Tremayne, Serjeant-at-Law, towards the latter part of the seventeenth century made some additions ; the Rev. H. H. Tremayne considerably altered the house in 1809 ; and his son, Mr. J. H. Tremayne, subsequently improved upon these alterations. The house, from an architectural point of view, has very little that is either striking or beautiful about it–it is severely plain, but large and substantial. Standing, as it does, however, amidst exceedingly beautiful scenery, Nature has more than fully compensated for defects which are after all merely a matter of detail.

The gardens are among the most interesting in this part of the county, at least three generations of Tremaynes fairly claiming the distinction of being described as ardent horticulturists. The late John Hearle Tremayne, father of the present owner, introduced a great variety of new improvements in the gardens, and made the drive one of the finest in the county, in 1832. Heligan may be almost described as the birthplace of Cornus capitata (Benthamia fragifera) : Sir Anthony Buller, in the early part of the century (about the year 1825, it is believed), gave Mr. J. H. Tremayne some seeds which he bought home from Nepaul, it(s) native

habitat. In the genial soil and climate of Heligan they grew and thrived amazingly, and when Mr. Tremayne made the drive in 1832, he planted this splendid tree on either side, with the result that from early summer till autumn the drive is simply a dense mass of white flowers. Bamboos are a strong and exceptionally interesting feature at Heligan, where they thrive, for the most part, in the wildest profusion. The largest piece is B. Simonii, which was planted about the year 1871 ; B. nobilis is also in large clumps, and appears to have been first planted here in 1874. Mr John Claude Tremayne, son of the present squire, and an enthusiastic amateur, has added all the varieties which he has been able to get in Europe during this last year or eighteen months, some of the rarer or less-known forms of this protean genus having been secured after much difficulty from a nurseryman in Italy.

The Indian Rhododendrons at Heligan are a great feature, and are well worth a journey all the way to Cornwall to see. The majority of the larger specimens were planted by Mr. John Tremayne some years ago. As the majority of these are figured in Sir Joseph Hooker's splendid folio, dealing with the Rhododendrons of the Sikkim Himalayas, it is most interesting to compare the plates in this work with the results of careful and intelligent culture in an entirely congenial habitat. The flowers are in nearly every instance finer, and the colours more brilliant. R. Griffthianum, syn. [Aucklandi], for instance, is an exceedingly fine plant, and the flowers, which measure from 3 to 5 inches and over in diameter, are, when first out, pinker than is usual with this species – in either its natural habitat or in other places. R. Thomsoni (Hooker, t. xi.), remarkable for the almost unrivalled deep blood-red colour and glossy surface of its flowers, is quite 25 feet high, and is probably the largest plant of this species in England. Sir Joseph Hooker describes this in its native habitat as a bush ranging from 6 to 10 feet high, "or in damp woods 15 feet high, but then spare and woody ;" at Heligan it attains to tree height without being either spare or woody. Of R. Falconeri, of which an illustration from a photograph taken by Mr. J. Claude Tremayne, is here given (fig 130, p.749 [not shown]), there are two large specimens ; the younger of these is about 15 years old ; and in April and May of this year it produced a record total of 258 flowering heads—one of these heads was $36\,{}^3/_4$ inches in circumference. This striking and distinct species, with its densely-packed flower heads, and beautiful Magnolia grandiflora-like leaves, is also figured by Sir Joseph Hooker ; but the plate does not give an adequate idea of the extraordinary beauty of this species as seen at Heligan. R. Hodgsoni (Hooker, tab. xv.), found at an elevation of from 10,000 feet to 12,000 feet in all the valleys of Sikkim, also thrives exceeding well at Heligan ; of the wood of this species, Sir Joseph Hooker states, cups, spoons, and ladles are made by the Bhoteas, and universally the little "Yak" saddle, by means of which the pack-loads are slung on the back of their animal. R. Campbelliae now (referred to R. arboreum) (fig 134, p.757 [not shown]) a flowering branch of which an illustration is here given, may be mentioned not only for its beauty, but for its free flowering character ; R. glaucum with its sweet-scented foliage, and R. formosum syn. Gibsoni, are all here, and all in great size. There are also two good-sized R. zeylanicum (arboreum), but they have never flowered.

A fine specimen of Eriobotrya japonica came originally from the south of France, and has acclimatised itself exceedingly well at Heligan, where it does best in a bank not far from water. Another plant, half-hardy elsewhere outside Cornwall, Hedychium Gardnerianum has been in its present place by the side of the stove-house for very many years ; it fruited last year, and Mr. Tremayne raised several plants from the seed. Berberidopsis corallina is also quite hardy ; Solanum jasminoides, which was actually touching the Berberidopsis, was killed two years ago, though other plants of the Solanum in other parts of the garden were not hurt. A very old plant of Camellia reticulata is still a profuse bloomer, and bears hundreds of huge flowers annually ; this past season it was a red blaze. Lapageria rosea flourishes, and produces flowers in great abundance; whilst Trapaeolum speciosum, a singularly beautiful plant, is equally hardy, and equally free flowering—essential points in its cultivation are plenty of room and a west wall.

There are about a dozen plants of Dicksonia antartica in the open at Heligan ; the largest was put in three or four years ago, and the remainder, which are comparatively small plants, were placed in the rockery a few months ago, and form an exceedingly charming addition to an artistic formation.

These plants were brought over from Sydney by Mr. J. Treseder, of Truro, and, so far, have shown no ill-effects of their long journey. I may here mention an exceptionally fine specimen plant of Chamaerops excelsa, which was planted by Mr. John Tremayne between 40 and 45 years ago, and is now over 20 feet in height ; there are several other plants of this graceful Palm, but none so large or so old as the above-mentioned.

There are very many interesting trees at Heligan, notably Pinus Ayacahuite ; this was given by Mr. J. Knight, of Chelsea to the late Mr. J. H. Tremayne, over 40 years ago, apparently soon after its introduction into this country, as it was first brought to England in 1840 by Hartweg for the Royal Horticultural Society. The illustration (fig.131, p. 751 [not shown]), from photograph taken by Mr. J. C. Tremayne, gives a very good idea of this very beautiful tree ; this specimen is believed to be the finest in England, and it is quite hardy. The illustration of the cones of this plant will also be interesting (fig.132, p.753 [not shown]), as they are of rare occurrence in this country. There is also a good specimen of Pinus montezumae, which was given to Mr. Tremayne by Mr. Jonathan Rashleigh of Menabilly a few years ago, and grown from seed

Tree ferns (Dicksonia antarctica) *in New Zealand*

saved by him. In a valley below the house is a very (?) specimen of Abies nobilis, about 66 feet high, girth 3 feet from ground, 6 feet 10 inches, at base 8 feet. This valley was quite a wild orchard until the present owner of Heligan began planting some rarer kinds of trees there ; it is now an arboretum of a most interesting character—indeed, it may be doubted whether there is a more successful garden lover in the county than Mr. John Tremayne.

Any reference to Heligan would be quite incomplete without mentioning the little enclosure know as Mrs. Tremayne's Garden. This is a very charming enclosure of about a quarter of an acre, filled with all kinds of old-fashioned flowers, which produce a gay succession from January to December—

"The daughters of the year,
One after one, thro' that still garden pass'd ;
Each garlanded with her peculiar flower
Danced into light, and died into the shade."

Mrs. Tremayne's garden more nearly approaches my own ideal of what an old English flower garden ought to be like than anything I have ever seen. It is certainly a most interesting and charming addition to the attractions of Heligan.

W. Roberts.

Mrs Tremayne's Garden, later known as the "Sun-Dial Garden". The photographs taken by Jack Tremayne which originally illustrated this article are not available. Alternatives taken by him at the same time appear on pages 16-18. Those above were taken a decade later by professional photographer, H. D. Wootton

Possibly on return from Mrs Tremayne's Garden, a lady of leisure in a by-gone era

The Hall in the 1890s, with exotic embellishment

The Drawing Room of Hon. Mrs. Tremayne, sweetly scented with lilies

The Library (to quote Damaris Tremayne) was the main family sitting room. "My great grand-parents' taste in furniture was evidently deplorable". Spot the lady vanishing, centre left

A correspondent's letter in the archive of the Pentewan Branch of the Old Cornwall Society reports that her ancestor was a kitchen maid at Heligan House in 1900. She had told of Sunday mornings when "ten or a dozen carriages … could be seen outside St Ewe Church, waiting for 'the gentry' to come out". She also said that there were "emus in the park". Squire John Tremayne was a passionate, if ageing, horticulturist and respected master of a handful of estates. His son Jack was already much involved in the development of the Gardens.

The 1901 Census takes us right to the heart of this world, recording the occupations of residents in Heligan House as well as on the surrounding tenant farms. Those specifically in the domestic service of the Tremaynes included: Groom, Stable boy, Coachman, Butler, General domestic servants, Laundress, Parlour maid, Housemaid, Dairymaid, Scullery maid, Housekeeper and, last but by no means least, Cook.

SACRED
TO THE MEMORY OF
JOHN TREMAYNE.
OF HELIGAN.
BORN APRIL 15TH.1825.
DIED APRIL 7TH.1901.

In 1901 John Tremayne died and Jack became Squire. For the next two decades he was head of the household (though not always resident), sustaining his family's enthusiasm for the new and the exotic and imprinting his aesthetic flair on everything. Both the Britannia boiler in the Head Gardener's Office and the 3-inch Ram Pump deep in the valley to the west at Corran were installed by Jack, in his quest for technology to support horticultural developments.

An inventory for Heligan House dated 1909 describes the reception rooms and some twenty-one bedrooms (all named after tenant farms on the Cornish estates belonging to the Tremaynes). At the back stairs was the servants' accommodation (including bedrooms for the footman and, significantly, the new chauffeur), along with all other facilities required to service the household... from Lamp Room and Boot-hole, Laundry and Ironing Room, to Scullery, Pantry and the all-important Kitchen.

The reception rooms were: Drawing Room, Red Room, Dining Room, Library, Smoking Room, Best Entrance, Hall with Staircase and Top Landing with Gallery. The inventory itemises furnishings and the vases required for decoration, for floral embellishment from the Gardens was without doubt in constant demand. The Flower Room held no less than 76 flower vases (mostly glass), the smallest of which were the 17 "Square-cut plain vases", possibly used beside each place at the dinner table.

Also in the Flower Room was some shelving, a 10 ft. by 3 ft. table, a large glazed flowerpot, a long-spout watercan and two square parrot cages. In the inventory the parrot cages were empty, but when there was a parrot in residence it had a place of honour, for in the Drawing Room was a "Mahogany Table for a Parrot". Spot him in the next photograph, out for exercise.

The Dining Room in 1905, with Drawing Room and Library beyond. Jack Tremayne is stamping his identity on House and Gardens

The walled Flower Garden (again, in 1905) has acquired a decorative lay-out, less suited to efficient productivity and harvest than those of the past. It even has a fountain in the Dipping Pool

While we recognise the Peach House in the distance behind an ornamental palm, the Paxton House on the left is mirrored by a third glass-house, which by 1911 had been replaced by a free-standing one with finials. That shown here is probably John Tremayne's Orchid House

Jack had been inspired by his continental travels to construct the Alpine Ravine as a Rockery in the 1890s

After his marriage was dissolved in 1903, he built the "Sun-Trap Garden" to remind him of his first love, Italy. The original kiwi was well established against the wall before the Great War

Wootton Postcards of Heligan, 1908

The separate achievements of Daguerre and Fox Talbot in 1839 marked the beginnings of photography as we know it. Herbert Darlow Wootton was born in 1877, the third in a line of five generations of professional photographers reaching back to the earliest days of the process. He was first employed by Walford and Co. in London, "Photographers in the Colours of Nature", in the last years of the nineteenth century and he fought in the Boer War in 1900. In 1906 he married and moved with his wife and his mother to Redruth, Cornwall, where he opened his own photographic studio. He subsequently photographed the gardens of Heligan and Enys as well as other places in the county, including the Royal Cornwall Show in 1909, attended by "The Prince and Princess".

He enlisted in 1915 and served in France, North Africa and Palestine; but during this period also worked as a photographer in the London area, taking pictures of Kew which he hand-coloured and marketed as a set of postcards – *The Darlow Collection*.

At the end of the Great War he was a military aircraft camera repairer.

"Wootton Postcards" hold considerable cachet here locally. I recently came across his grand-daughter, who showed us the letter from John Claude Lewis Tremayne which commissioned H. D. Wootton to make the very first collection of postcards of Heligan (*see right and over*). What an extraordinary accident of fate. Her mother, as a teenager, had even painted the view from Heligan House down into the Jungle.

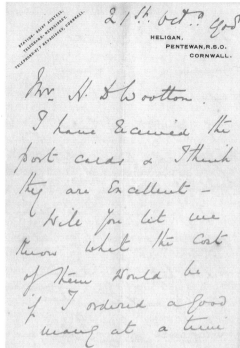

Above *H. D. Wootton as a young man*
Right *A letter from Jack Tremayne,
dated 1908, commissions Wootton
to provide "hundreds" of postcards
of Heligan.* Samples below, clockwise:
*"A Peep over the Flowers", "Heligan,
Pentewan, Cornwall", "New Zealand",
"Heligan from S. E.", "The New Garden"*

Some hundreds I mean – In some cases I should like say fifty of each, if we could come to terms –

If you will let me know about this I will let you know the quantity that I require – I see no reason why the cards should be private & I have no objection whatever to their being sold to the public –

I should like some more done in the spring – when the flowers are out

Yours faithfully

John Tremayne.

HELIGAN, PENTEWAN, CORNWALL.

HELIGAN, NEW ZEALAND

HELIGAN, THE NEW GARDEN

HELIGAN, FROM S.E.

The Tremayne archive includes both "Wootton Postcards" and many fascinating photographs taken by Jack Tremayne throughout this period
Above *Agapanthus inside box hedging, against a south-facing wall*

Above *The* Rhododendron falconeri *outside the Head Gardener's Office is already some 50 years old, grown from seed collected in Sikkim by Sir Joseph Hooker*

Opposite Ginkgo biloba, *viewed through the dramatic plantings of the New Zealand Garden, also stands proud, on Eastern Ride*

Conifers and exotics, as well as camellias and rhododendrons, already adorn the borders of both Rides in the Northern Gardens

This route led away to the south from Heligan House, laced with hydrangeas which brought vibrant summer colour to the Gardens

"The Orchard", as it had been, became the focus for an impressive diversity of architectural plants introduced from at least five continents

A bazaar at Heligan, with guests in Edwardian dress

"This is a part of Heligan taken when the bazaar was" writes Ethel to her Aunt, Mary Moyse; the card was posted on October 18th, 1911

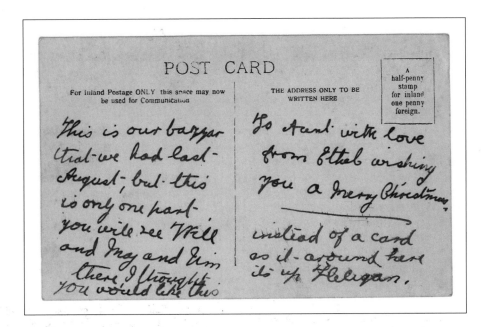

POST CARD

For Inland Postage ONLY this space may now be used for Communication

THE ADDRESS ONLY TO BE WRITTEN HERE

A half-penny stamp for inland one penny foreign.

This is our bazaar that we had last August; but this is only one part you will see Will and May and Jim there I thought you would like this

To Aunt with love from Ethel wishing you a merry Christmas instead of a card as it around here its up Heligan.

Additional archive for our Second Edition includes these two fabulous images showing a bazaar held at Heligan, probably in the summer of 1911. These postcards are not identifiable as Wootton's; but they are of great interest because they are the first we have come across showing people at leisure in the garden. Ethel comments "You will see Will and May and Jim there", but we have no idea which of those outside the House are they, nor whether any of the four of them were staff.

The photograph *(opposite)* taken beside probably the Top Pond in the "Orchard" (now known as the Jungle) shows at least six adults and a child, some forming possibly a family group looking north, back up towards Heligan House. *(See the bottom of page 25 to appreciate their view, with even the swans back in position!)* Whereas photos of this area on page 31 show a variety of coniferous, exotic and architectural trees and plants, this angle features the rhododendrons we recognise today, already of considerable size.

At last we have a picture of life at Heligan, albeit on a special occasion.

Chapter Two LOST GARDENERS

So much for archive and images of Heligan in her golden era... Heligan's last resident Squire – and garden creator – was not only a plantsman with flair, but also a sufficiently accomplished photographer to have his plant portraits published in *The Gardeners' Chronicle* in 1896, within years of the first half-tone reproductions appearing in newspapers. We also know that he commissioned views of the Pleasure Grounds from professional photographer H. D. Wootton in 1908 and was proud enough of the subject matter to order postcards... treasures indeed to impress even now – and to convey us back into the past.

However, there appears to be no photographic record of the strictly functional, productive areas in this period before the Great War and none, except the marvel below, has come to light of the garden staff in their workplaces. One can but guess the roles of the characters in this fabulous set piece – and what might have prompted 'the sitting'.

At Heligan, working areas and working people were apparently not generally considered appropriate subjects. Although clearly benign patrons, the Tremaynes kept their outdoor staff at arms length through a structure of supervision and reporting overseen by the Head Gardener and Farm Steward, who linked them with the requirements of the family. The photograph opposite was brought to us some years ago by a descendant of one of Heligan's head gardeners of the period, a certain Thomas W. Preece, who is the gentleman sitting without a hat. The 1901 Census records him as a 45-year-old gardener living at Pengrugla, outside Higher Lodge, with his wife and four young children. He was Head Gardener 1903-07 and later lived at Palm Cottage, the Head Gardener's residence beside the Sundial Garden. The man sitting next to Preece, with a long white beard, may be Samuel Mutton. The credit on the back of the original photograph (believed to have been taken around 1900) was to a Mr F. Dalby-Smith of The Studio, Mevagissey.

As chance meetings with relatives of past Heligan staff continued, we were privileged to establish contact with a Mr Ken Paynter, whose grandfather, uncle and father had all worked at Heligan. The 1901 Census records the young family living at Blow-the-Winds (a cottage just outside St Ewe and not far from the main Drive to Heligan House), with William, aged 38, a stone mason. Ken produced a family photo from which we were able to confirm that the tall dark gentleman on the far left of the staff group photo *(opposite)* was in fact his grandfather, William Paynter.

We understand from unprompted letters that a certain Nimrod Davy was possibly the bowler-hatted head gardener, featured on the postcard of New Zealand *(page 27)*. R. W. Norman held the position in 1909 and 1911–13. His enlightening letter of reference for gardener Diggory Abbott to take promotion elsewhere is reproduced on the following page. It is clear that, notwithstanding the continuity of numerous local families over generations, it was also part of life that staff would come and go, both in the search for temporary employment on meagre seasonal wages and to secure promotion. See the career of Harry Williams recorded on page 15. In Edwardian England, even within Cornwall, there were plenty of other estates like Heligan. *The Horticultural Directory* records that H. Griffin was head gardener in 1914.

Above Introducing the Paynter Family – stern faces in the early era of photography for the general public. William, the head of the household, was to be in service at Heligan for sixty years. He and his wife, Eliza Jane, had four sons, William, Richard, Frederick and Ernest (as yet unborn), and three daughters, Ethel, Minnie and Alice. Here, Fred sits on his mother's knee

The Gardens.
HELIGAN
PENTEWAN, R.S.O.
CORNWALL.

STATION: ST. AUSTELL, G.W.R.
TELEGRAMS:—" MEVAGISSEY."
TELEPHONE:—No. 7, MEVAGISSEY.

14 Dec. 1912.

Dear Sir.

Diggory Abbott was employed principally out of doors here, There was a re-arrangement of the staff when I came and Abbott was kept as leading hand outside, previous to that he did duty under glass as well —

He has a good knowledge of Peaches — Vines, We have not cultivated oranges here, only so far as a few exist during favourable seasons in open air —

He has assisted in the pruning of all the general run of fruit trees, training and tying of the same —

We grow good Peaches and he assisted in planting young trees, in lifting and root pruning of them, dressing of the borders and thinning shoots and fruit as a lot of this was done in bad weather and used him for it more than other outside men —

He can grow melons, and also Begonias Gloxinias and the usual run of annual flowering plants and bulbs —

The charge of a small stove also he could manage

In regard to men he has had charge of two or three men at times and has managed them well in carrying out different work and should be able to do so when he has full charge of them.

I cannot say much about decoration as I have not used him for it at all — He made up a wreath or two very fairly but that is all I have seen of his work in that respect

He knows how to keep up a succession of Flowers and Vegetables, and once he gets a gauge of what you require should be able to do so well —

This is a clear as I can answer your questions respecting him, and anything further I shall be pleased to do if required

Yours Sincerely

R.W. Norman

It is small bits of documentary evidence as much as photographs that have helped us put together a picture of the past and not least among the random bits of archive that remain are the Heligan Estate Labour Books kept between April 1914 and July 1917. The first is a beautifully bound book covered in red and blue marbled paper, each double-page spread recording the detail of a week's labour in a fine flowing hand. On 8th August 1914 there are 22 staff and the previous month's wage bill is a total of £105. 8s. 2d. The highest pay was around 4/- per day and the lowest around 2/8 (plus 2d. for each mole trapped and 1d. for each rat). Regular activities included much carting of building materials and hauling of timber and peat, with all sorts of deliveries and collections to and from St Austell station. "Roofs" seem to have been a constant preoccupation around the whole estate, with many tenant farms and cottages apparently included at the squire's expense and itemised in the workbooks. About five or six staff (then approximately a quarter of all outside workers) appear to have been devoted to Garden activities, but other regular workplaces were: Orchard, Woods, Quarry, Stable and Mansion. Someone was always allocated to "Back Door". Maintenance of the Drive was of paramount concern, with numerous staff devoted to it week on week.

This routine had probably been played out for years and certainly A. Smaldon had secured his place at the top of each page with the highest wage. Over the months his attention revolved around: Mansion, Garden frames, painting "Lights", Peach house and Carnation house, Motor body (and, in 1916, "Yacht"!). William Paynter had been joined in employment at Heligan by two of his sons; Richard (28), a carpenter, and Frederick (21) – Ken's father – a mason, like William. William was on a wage of 4/- a day and is recorded working on: Cheesewarne roof, Garden roofs, Motor house, Sawing and Mixing lime (amongst many other things).

Little could any of them have appreciated how the outbreak of the First World War was to change their world. All summer the turmoil in Europe had been brewing and on 4th August 1914 Britain declared war on Germany. This was in immediate response to Germany's declaration of war on Russia and France and the German invasion of Belgium.

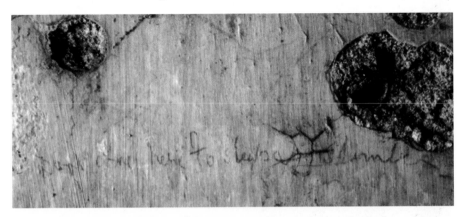

The message on the Thunderbox wall is "Don't come here to sleep or slumber"

	NAME	MONDAY. 3	TUESDAY. 4	WEDNES
a.	A. Snelston	Shop	House Kettle	benim
12.	R. Paynter	benimney	benimney Taking down	Shopin
7	J. Gane	Sharping saw	Band erection	benim
7	W. Paynter	Stn for slate	House Kettle	benim
7.	F. Paynter	Absent	Station for slate	
J.	J. Holman	Stn for slate	"	Stn noth
J.	J. Trevenna	"	Farm	Cutting
J.	W. H. Bale	Narrow	"	Back
W.	A. Rundle	Quarry	Quarry	Quar
a.	W. Hunken			
11.	H. Pascoe	Cutting Lawns	Weeding	Clean
H.	W. King		Farm	Cutting
W.	J. Rowe	Kitchen gdn	Kitchen gdn	Kitchen
J.	J. Sey	Weeding beds	Weeding	Weedin
J.	J. Mill	Rock gdn	"	
H.	H. J. Griffin	House	House	Hous
W.	W. Bamford	Bothy	Bothy	Bo
C.	C. Moss	Rock gdn	Potting	Borde
O.	O. Gray	Back door		
O.	W. Perry	Quarry	Quarry	Qua

THURSDAY. 6	FRIDAY. 7	SATURDAY. 8	No. of Days	Price per day	Insurance Stamps	AMOUNT £	s.	d.
	Piecework.							
Lone Kestle	Lone Kestle	Lone Kestle	2½	4/	3		10	X
Trevinney	Trevinney	" "	5	3/8	3		18	4 X
Sharping saw	Gate etc	Sawing	6	3/6	3	1	1	X
Trelean	Tregarton	Tregarton	5	3/10	3		19	2 X
Trevinney	" "	" "	5	3/4	3		16	8 X
Estate carting	Estate carting	Sawing	6	3/4	3	1		/
Farm	Cutting lawns	" "	6	3/	3		18	/
Back door	Various	" "	6	3/	3		18	X
Quarry	Quarry.	Quarry.			3	Piecework		
"					3	"		
Cutting lawns	Cutting lawns	Sawing	6	3/	3		18	X
Farm		" "	6	3/	3		18	X
Kitchen gdn	Kitchen gdn	Kitchen gdn	6	2/10	3		17	X
Weeding	Weeding	Various Potting shed	6	2/6	4		15	X
"	" "	" "	6	1/4			8	X
Houses	Houses	House	6	3/4	3	1	.	/
Bothy	Bothy	Bothy	6	2/	3		12	X
Borders	Borders	Potting shed	6	4/2	3	1	5	X
			6	2/10	3		17	X
					3	Piecework		
Quarry	Quarry.	Quarry						
					4/10	14	11	10

In due course Squire Jack Tremayne left the Mansion and moved up to Croan, another Tremayne property, on the North Coast near Wadebridge, which had been assigned to his married sister. The workbooks record three two-day visits to Croan by staff to deliver plants. Heligan House was handed over for use as a military hospital, offering convalescence for wounded officers.

At the beginning of October 1914, less than two months after August payday, the wage bill is down to £60. 13s. 8d. for only 16 staff. By January 1915, the bill was only £45. 17s. 10d. for 12 remaining. Until this point there is no specific mention of any departures, but on Monday 1st March it was recorded that F. Paynter "Left to enlist". Three weeks later, while his colleague J. James was "Making run for young emus", W. King "Enlisted"; although he is back on the books by the end of the year. By the middle of 1915 the records are still in the same handwriting but significantly briefer, noting work locations only. The 12 remaining staff are obviously required to be flexible to ensure the Garden stays in production, with its labour costs now accounting for a third of the total. On Monday 8th May 1916, after conscription was introduced in Britain, A. Smaldon "tried to enlist direct", but then seems to carry on working – maybe he was deemed unfit or too old to join up. In December 1916, when the second marble covered labour book is full, it is replaced by an economy one with a plain cardboard cover. Payday in February 1917 is the last record in the same handwriting. Someone else takes over and finds it impossible to keep track. It appears he does not know what is going on, with much crossing out and changing of recorded work places. By March 1917 the Garden accounts for more than half the labour; the three old stalwarts J. Ley, J. Mills and J. Rowe, who were gardeners/labourers in 1914 and no doubt before, have been joined by L. Dyer and J. Brown, recorded as "moving in" in April 1916.

By July 1917 there are only 8 out of 22 outdoor (garden and maintenance) staff left at Heligan and there are no more entries in the labour book, although verbal anecdote mentions a Hilda Lobb, aged 14, becoming a gardener in 1917.

Gentle research undertaken over the past decade shows that at least eight people who had worked in the gardens or estate at Heligan departed the relatively secure haven of their known world and signed up as: "Sons of the Empire, who on land and sea, beneath the sea and in the air, risk their lives for Imperial Honour, Righteousness, and Loyalty to Allies".

MESSAGE FROM LORD KITCHENER TO THE SOLDIERS OF THE BRITISH EXPEDITIONARY FORCE

You are ordered abroad as a soldier of the King to help our French comrades against the invasion of a common enemy… In this new experience you may find temptation both in wine and women. You must entirely resist both temptations, and, while treating all women with perfect courtesy, you should avoid any intimacy. Do your duty bravely. Fear God. Honour the King.

ST. AUSTELL STAR AND CORNISH ADVERTISER – Thursday August 6, 1914

THE WAR

MEVAGISSEY RESERVISTS DEPARTURE.

LOCAL INDUSTRIES AFFECTED.

1,000 CLAYWORKERS GIVEN NOTICE.

The one topic of conversation during the past week has been the war and the black outlook seems to have cast a gloom over almost everything. The crisis was brought more vividly than ever to the minds of all who beheld the departure of the Naval reservists from St. Austell station last Sunday evening. Here were assembled a body of bronzed men numbering over a hundred who form a portion of those upon whom England depends for the safety of her shores. No one knew their inward feelings but altogether they appeared to be in good spirits and fully prepared, if necessary, to fight for their King and the country they love so well. Hundreds of people were present to give these sea-faring men of Mevagissey and Gorran a hearty send-off and as a special train containing a large number of reservists from other western towns steamed into the station there was some lusty cheering by the crowd which had assembled not only on the platform but along Palace Road, over the bridge and in the station entrance. There were hearty handshakes and farewell greetings and in a few minutes amidst further cheering husbands, sons and friends were parted for an indefinite period.

Writing from Mevagissey our correspondent says :

Mevagissey is hardly likely to forget the first Sunday in August 1914, that date being very deeply marked in the annals of her history, as the day which witnessed the calling up of her reservists for actual service. A very large percentage of Mevagissey men have been or still are, in the naval reserve, and when on Sunday the men in commission were called out, the town was speedily in a commotion. The ringing of a bell by the town-crier and the call to reservists to turn out, was the first intimation of the news, and although since the calling up of the coastguards, which occurred last week, the possibility of this event taking place has been discussed, the suddenness of this early morning call was none the less unexpected. Most of the men were in bed, but in an incredibly short time everyone was astir, some even in reserve costume in a few minutes, which showed that things had been in readiness.

During the morning hours the scene was a busy one, reservists attending the coastguard station to sign their papers and for medical examination. It was found that out of the large number of men in the reserve in commission belonging to Mevagissey, only about forty-eight were at present in the place, the missing ones being absent at sea or yachting, the number yachting being greater this year than usual owing to poor fishing seasons. About mid-day the little company started from the Town Bridge, being sent off by one of the biggest crowds of their townspeople that ever assembled. Headed by the town band they marched to the top of New Road-hill, where Great Western motors were waiting to convey them to St. Austell. There were many sad faces among those who watched their husbands, sons or brothers march away, for although the reservists themselves were so cheerful, those who were left behind could not help but think what might happen before the gallant little band came home again, or whether they would all come back.

It is impossible to comprehend how they coped with their awesome challenge, but the following *DAILY THOUGHTS* we chanced on were published in *The Happy Warrior* (over 200,000 copies issued by 1917, with a Foreword by Field-Marshal Earl Roberts, K.G.) "for all who are serving their country". They give us a shocking impression of stern imperialist morality and the personal sacrifice expected.

"Thou hast heard, O my soul, the sound of the trumpet, the alarm of war. Who is on the Lord's side?" – Jer.iv.19; Exod. Xxxii. 26.

"What mean ye to weep and to break my heart? The will of the Lord be done." – Acts xxi. 13, 14.

"The Lord watch between me and thee, when we are absent one from another!" – Gen. xxxi. 49.

"O LORD our God, who art in every place, from Whom no space or distance can ever separate us, we know that those that are absent from each other are present with thee. We pray Thee to have in Thy holy keeping those dear ones from whom we are now separated, that bound together by Thy love, in the communion of Thy Spirit we may surely meet again, on earth if it be Thy will, and if not, at the Resurrection of the just; through JESUS CHRIST our LORD."

"O THOU, the Watcher and the Holy One, be with Thy servant through the hours of darkness. Uphold me by Thine own presence. Keep far from me every danger. Deliver me from fearfulness and let not sleep overpower me. Perfect Thy strength in my weakness that I may faithfully fulfil my charge and whensoever Thou comest may be found watching."

"Ye approach this day unto battle against your enemies: let not your hearts faint, fear not, and do not tremble; for the LORD your GOD is He that goeth with you, to fight for you."

"Oh ALMIGHTY GOD, Whose power no creature is able to resist; strengthen us by Thy grace that by the constancy of our faith, even unto death, we may glorify Thy holy Name, and being steadfast in faith, joyful through hope, and rooted in love, we may so pass the waves of this troublesome world, that finally we may come to the land of everlasting life; through JESUS CHRIST our LORD."

"In the midst of life we are in death; of whom may we seek for succour, but of Thee, O LORD? O LORD GOD most holy, O LORD most mighty, O holy and most merciful Saviour, deliver us not into the bitter pains of eternal death; suffer us not, at our last hour, for any pains of death, to fall from Thee. By Thy Cross and Passion save us, O LORD."

LORD, when with dying lips my prayer is said,
Grant that in faith Thy kingdom I may see;
And, thinking on Thy Cross and thorn-crowned head,
May breathe my parting words "Remember me."
Remember me; and ere I pass away,
Speak Thou the assuring Word that sets us free,
And make Thy promise to my heart "Today
Thou too shalt rest in Paradise with Me." Maclagan.

"The fruit of the Spirit is peace. Peace I leave with you, My peace I give unto you. Let not your heart be troubled, neither let it be afraid." – Gal. v.22; S. John xiv. 27.

About 800,000 British troops died or were lost (presumed dead) in the Great War of 1914-18; of the Allies, only Russia and France suffered greater losses. UK national statistics show about one in eight of those who enlisted were lost. In total, over 8 million died, with 20 million wounded. The unspeakable conditions on the Western Front also promoted the transmission and virulence of the influenza virus, or "Spanish Flu", that reached pandemic proportions in 1918-19 and killed even more than were lost in battle. With the incomprehensible scale of human tragedy and the decimation of a generation of menfolk, it is no wonder the scars of the period remain.

Passchendaele, Pilckem Ridge, near Boesinghe, 1.8.1917
Q5935. Photograph courtesy of the Imperial War Museum

43

Mark 1 Tank C Company broken down on way to Thiepval, Somme, 1916
Q2486. Photograph courtesy of the Imperial war Museum

Passchendaele, Battle of Poelcapelle. 18-pounder gun near Langemark, 16.10.1917
Q3007. Photograph courtesy of the Imperial War Museum

Chateau Wood, Passchendaele, 29.10.1917
E(AUS)1220. Photograph courtesy of the Imperial War Museum

Desolation on the crest of Pozières Ridge (The Somme)
E(AUS)0015. Photograph courtesy of the Imperial War Museum

William Robins Guy

William was one of a family of eleven. He lived in Gorran Haven with his parents, John and Annie Louisa, in the home of his maternal grandfather, Jacob Robins, who was a fisherman. The children helped their parents grow vegetables on their three allotments and William was particularly keen on gardening. He started work when he was fourteen and by 1914 had two part-time jobs, one in Gorran and the other in the Vegetable Garden at Heligan. His younger brother, Philip Guy, told us that he also loved wildlife and music and was saving money to buy an organ. He eventually had enough to acquire a small American harmonium, which he never got the chance to play. He volunteered when war broke out and enlisted in the Duke of Cornwall's Light Infantry, serving as a Corporal with the 1st/5th Battalion. Of all the Heligan staff who served in the war, William Guy held the most senior position in either of the forces.

Philip never forgot the last time he saw his brother. It was 1918 and William, aged 22, was on leave from the Western Front. As always, he attended the Methodist Chapel in Gorran. "We used to go to chapel together and I'd hold his hand and look up at him in his uniform and think what a fine fellow he was," Philip said. "But that last time we shared a hymn book as usual, and I could barely read it because Will's hand was shaking so much. I didn't understand why at the time."

William Guy died sometime between 13th and 17th April, 1918 (the records vary). The D.C.L.I. had been defending, and holding, a section of the front line against a determined German advance at Le Sart, south of Lille. His body was never found. He is remembered on Panel 68 of the Loos Memorial, which forms the side and back walls of Dud Corner Military Cemetery. 20,000 of the fallen who have no known grave are commemorated here.

"I never remember him as anything but content", said Philip. "He was a gentle man. After the war I went to see an uncle of ours and I noticed he had a linnet in a cage on the kitchen table. I asked him about it and he told me, 'It was your Will that found it crippled in a hedge, nursed it back to health and gave it to our daughter. He was always fond of her'."

Charles Ball

Philip Guy also spoke of another man, Charles Ball, who had worked alongside his older brother William at Heligan, attended the same Gorran Methodist Chapel, and lost his life in the same German Spring Offensive of 1918. They are remembered together on the St Goran Church memorial plaque *(previous page, bottom)*. Of 106 men from Gorran parish who served their country at this time, William and Charles were two of 16 who gave their lives.

Charles Ball was born in 1876 to Frederick and Eliza Ann who also lived in Gorran Haven, where his father was a fisherman. He was a huge man, over 6 feet tall, and being very strong, he worked as a roadman. But he was apparently a gentle giant, known to be religious, with a beautiful singing voice. He would have been much older than other Heligan staff when he enlisted, leaving behind his wife Laura with their young daughter, Ena.

He joined the 10th Battalion of the Worcestershire Regiment as a Private and was serving near the town of Bapaume on the Somme when he was wounded in battle on 27th March 1918. Suffering severe shell wounds to his chest and arm, he was evacuated to the Canadian Military Hospital at Etaples. His wife Laura was immediately notified, but her request to visit her husband was denied. He was too badly injured to write home himself but hospital staff relayed messages: "His chief anxiety is about you and his child. He prays for you constantly and tells me how glad he would be to have the privilege of going with both of you to chapel once more."

Charles died of his wounds on 3rd April 1918, aged 42. A nurse wrote to his widow: "He spoke of you and his regret at not being able to see you again. He was so good and patient all the time..." He was buried in Etaples Military Cemetery alongside approximately 11,000 others.

Clockwise from top:
The Widow's Penny or Death Plaque (a million of which were issued within Commonwealth countries) and a letter from the King, received by Laura Ball; the British War Medal issued (amongst others) for Charles Ball's service to His Majesty's Forces; Etaples Military Cemetery; the gravestone of Charles Ball

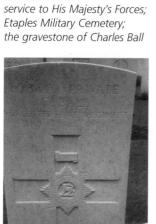

Charles Dyer

The 1901 Census shows Charles (Snr.) and Ellen Jane Dyer living at Heligan Mill, with Charles, the oldest of three children, aged 17, recorded as a "Gardener (not domestic)". Unusually, he appears also to be listed in the same census as living at Heligan, aged 17, as a servant to the Head of the family, position "Gardener, Domestic".

Both his father and his uncle worked out of Mevagissey as fishermen. At the outbreak of war it appears that Charles was already serving as a member of the Royal Naval Reserve, so he would have been among the first to have been called up. On board HMS "Charybdis", the flagship of the 12th Cruiser Squadron, it seems in September 1915 he would have been involved in a collision which subsequently left the vessel laid up in Bermuda.

HMS "Charybdis"   HMT "Essex", sister ship to "Rosa"

By Christmas 1915 Seaman Dyer was serving on board His Majesty's Trawler "Rosa", on Northern Patrol. This steam trawler had been hired by the Navy for mine sweeping duties. "Rosa", at 125ft. long, was not a big vessel, but she was fitted with a 3-pounder gun mounted on her foredeck and is believed to have seen action in the Battle of Jutland in 1916.

At some point later in the war Charles was wounded and moved to a naval hospital at HMS "Pembroke", a shore-based facility at Chatham Dockyard, from which he disappeared. He was registered as a deserter and his wife, Annie Elizabeth, and three children had to suffer the stigma attached to such a charge. Some time after his disappearance a skeleton was found in some woods; the wedding ring identified it as being that of Charles Dyer. The Navy then removed him from the deserters' list and granted Annie the widow's pension she deserved. It didn't heal the pain. Their grandson Perren Dyer recalled that she would always burst into tears at the mention of his name and wore black until she died in 1966, aged 84.

Seaman Charles Dyer's death is recorded as 24th May 1918. He was 35 years old. His grave is in the cemetery of St Peter's Church, Mevagissey and he is remembered on the village war memorial. One of his sons is known to have worked at Heligan during the Second World War.

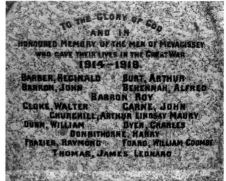

Leonard Warne

Leonard was born in 1890, the son of John and Anna Marie Warne, who were recorded living at Trelewack, St Ewe, a tenant farm on the Heligan Estate, in the 1901 Census. He was one of nine children and the memories of him have been reported by Hugh, a nephew who never knew him but whose own father, Richard, was one of Leonard's older brothers. Leonard worked at Heligan and was a keen gardener, cutting hedges and lawns, looking after the glasshouses and digging vegetables. He then emigrated to Canada and worked on a ranch there, just before the outbreak of war.

He returned to England and volunteered to become a Sapper in the Royal Engineers. Little is known of his war service but he served on the Western Front, where he was severely wounded in the back and invalided home. He arrived at Plymouth on board a hospital ship and was taken to a military hospital in the city. Hugh's father remembered visiting his brother Leonard and seeing him wearing his 'hospital blues'. He never recovered from his wounds and died on 21st April 1920.

Leonard Warne's gravestone is a granite cross placed in a recumbent position in the churchyard of St Bartholomew's, Lostwithiel, near to where his parents had moved in 1905. He is also remembered on the war memorial at St Ewe *(below)*.

Percy Carhart

Percy Carhart is the second of Heligan's outdoor staff to be remembered on the St Ewe memorial and roll of honour. He is also remembered on the war memorial at Veryan. His loss is mourned to this day.

Percy was born on 24th February 1898 in the village of St Kew, between Wadebridge and Camelford, the son of railway worker, James Carhart and his wife, Emma. He had two older brothers and two sisters. At some point they moved south to Pengrugla, the small hamlet outside the gates to Heligan House. There is also a family record

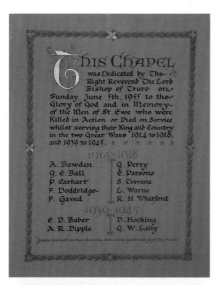

Veryan War Memorial

of him living locally at Trevilveth Farm, Caerhays. When he enlisted in Truro in June 1916 he was 18 years old and gave his occupation as a labourer.

Percy was attached to the 1st Battalion Duke of Cornwall's Light Infantry as Private No. 36117 and his regimental records show him as 5ft. 3$\frac{1}{2}$ins. tall, the minimum height limit for joining the army being 5ft. 3ins. He weighed 7st. 3lbs. and as an infantryman would have been expected to carry personal equipment weighing 4st. 5lbs. When he left home he told his brother, Wilfred, "I will never see you again." An enormous framed photograph of Percy in his D.C.L.I. uniform *(opposite)* was to hang in Wilfred's front room for many years, movingly recalled by both his daughter and grand daughter, who grew up under its spell. Percy's innocence and courage shine out. Wilfred himself was not fit to go to war; but Percy's other brother enlisted – and returned with medals for bravery.

Percy's Battalion was posted to Ypres in Flanders and fought in perhaps the most horrific of all First World War battles, Passchendaele. He appears to have been wounded in the fighting north of Gheluvelt. The official history of the D.C.L.I. records that, "The end of October was a veritable nightmare. In the front line conditions were truly terrible. It was bad enough to be shelled and potted at all day... it was necessary also to be on the alert lest you slipped down the slippery, muddy side of the shell-hole into the slime and mud and filthy water at the bottom." Nobody knows exactly how Percy died, aged 19, on 30th October 1917, and he has no known grave.

Percy Carhart is nonetheless commemorated on the 'Memorial to the Missing' at Tyne Cot, near Passchendaele in Belgium (Panels 80 to 82 and 163a). Tyne Cot is the largest Commonwealth overseas war cemetery in the world, containing nearly 12,000 graves. Percy is one of another 35,000 UK and New Zealand men who have no known grave, but were killed or died of wounds in this area, and who are named on this very extensive memorial to the missing, which runs along the top side of the cemetery.

MER DU NORD

Percy Carl

William Guy

Charles Ball

ANGLETERRE
Minster
North Foreland
Ramsgate
Sandwich
Goodnestone
...ham
Deal
Northbourn
Ewell
Kingsdown
South Foreland
St Margarets
DOVER (DOUVRES)
...gham
East Weer Bay
...gate
FOLKESTONE
East Point

PAS DE CALAIS

CALAIS
Sangatte
Wissant
Cap Gris Wez
Andresselles
Escalles
Ferques
Marquise
Wimille
Wimereux
BOULOGNE
le Portel
Outreau
Hesdigneul
Hardelot
la Canche
Etaples
le Touquet-
Paris Plage
Merlimont
Berck-s-M
Baie d'Authie
Fort Mahon
Quend Plage
Pte de St Quentin
le Crotoy
Baie de la Somme
le Hourdel
Cayeux
St Valéry

English Channel
MANCHE

Gd Fort-Philippe
Gravelines
Merck
Canal
Audruicq
Guînes
Ardres
Nielles
Licques
Bonningues
St OMER
Surques
Lumbres
Arques
Desvres
la Liane
Nielles-l-Bon
Thérouanne
HAZEBROUCK
Samer
Fauquembergues
Aire
Enquin
Frencq
Hucqueliers
Inxent
Neuville
Fruges
Créquy
Heuchin
Marles
Norrent-
fontès
l'Estrée Blanche
Auchy
MONTREUIL
Beaurainville
Anvin
Lespinoy
Rang du Fliers
Vertan
Campagne-l-Hn
Hesdin
le Parcq
St POL
Brias
Nempont
Dompierre
Rue
Filièvre
Labroye
Auxi-le-Chau
Hiermont
Canchy
Crécy en Ponthieu
Nouvion en P.
Frévent
Wavans
Occoches
Wavans
le Souich
PAS DE C...
DOULLENS

DUNKERQUE
Malo-les-Bains
Fort des Dunes
Ras Mdile
Bray D...
Zuydcoote
Pte Synthe
Loon Plage
Cal
Coudekerque
Bergues
Bierne
Bourbourg-Ville
Oost...
Bourb Campagne
Bollezeele
Wormhout
Cassel
Watten
St Momelin
Bavinchove
...

Wattrelos
THérouanne
Lys
Ternoise
la Canche
l'Authie
la Canche
Etr...

OSTENDE

Weerdamme
Den haan
Westcappelle
Dudzeele
Oostburg
Aardenburg
Philippine
Axel
BRUGES
EECLOO
Sluisk

Nieuport
Slype
Zandwoorde
Ghistelles
Maldeghem
Oedelem
Waerschoot
Somergem
Evergem
Lokere
Ochris

FURNES
DIXMUDE
Cortemark
Woummen
Thourout
Winghene
Nevele
Deynze
GAND
Gentbrugge

ROULERS
Staden
Hooglede
Ardoye
Denterghem
Ingelmunster
Nazareth
Oosterzeele
Nerzwalm

YPRES
Langhemarco
Iseghem
Passchendaele
Ledeghem
Harlebeke
COURTRAI
Waereghem
Wortegem
Sotteghem

Poperinghe
Abeele
Zonnebeke
Gheluwelt
Moorseele
Sweveghem
Rolleghem
Avelghem
AUDENARDE
Berchem
Renaix
Nederwakel
Flobecq
Lessines

Bailleul
Messines
Wervicq
Comines
MENIN
Mouscron
Dottignies
Amougies
Ellezelles
Celles
Frasnes
ATH

Armentières
TOURCOING
Quesnoy
ROUBAIX
Wattrelos
Kain
TOURNAI
Leuze
Chièvres

LILLE
Haubourdin
Loos
Wavrin
Lannoy
Templeuve
Bouvines
Cysoing
Antoing
Péruwelz
Quevaucamps
Ghislain
Boussu

BÉTHUNE
la Bassée
Don
Seclin
Fumes
Ft de Maulde
St Amand
Condé

LENS
Carvin
Pont-à-Marcq
Mons-en-Pévèle
Orchies
Marchiennes
Anzin
VALENCIENNES

Liévin
Vimy
Henin Liétard
DOUAI
Somain
Scarpe
Quiévrain
MAU

ARRAS
DENAIN
Bouchain
NORD

CAMBRAI
Solesmes

Archibald Smaldon

The Heligan Labour Book records that, after trying to enlist on Monday 8th May 1916, Archibald Smaldon was soon back at work at Heligan. We know little about him except that the 1901 Census describes him as a carpenter, aged 19, living in Alwington, Devon with his parents and younger sister. His father was a gamekeeper and it is possible he worked on one of the Tremayne estates locally, thus qualifying for transfer to Heligan. Archibald would have been about 34 when he tried to enlist and had probably, because of his age, waited until conscription was introduced. The Labour Book, however, records a second attempt two weeks later, on 24th May 1916 and we have a copy of his Medal Record Card showing that he joined up as a Private in the Machine Gun Corps and later served in the Royal Engineers. He was awarded the British War Medal and the Inter-Allied Victory Medal, issued to all those who survived service in the war.

Albert Rowe

Albert Rowe's signature *(opposite, above)* remains more legible now than any other on the lime-washed walls of the Thunderbox Room at Heligan. Records show that he was born in St Austell in 1900 and at the age of 6 months was living with his parents in Charlestown. Enlistment books at the D.C.L.I. Museum in Bodmin record him joining the 4th Reserve Battalion on 8th November 1918, only three days before war ended.

The Commonwealth War Graves Commission has recorded him as dying on the same day. He was only 18 and never saw action. He was buried in St Austell Cemetery on 14th November 1918, where there is a C.W.G.C. headstone in his name. It is understood that Albert was already very ill with pneumonia when he enlisted and it is possible that he died from the flu pandemic.

Frederick Paynter

And finally, a story of certainty and good fortune; no wonder this is the one that has been shared with mutual enjoyment over the past few years, since we first met Ken Paynter, son of Fred. The knowledge has been handed down and the memories are first-hand. Ken's grandfather, William, was the backbone of the Heligan staff for more than half a century, appearing in the staff photo of 1900 and securing employment for two of his sons when they were old enough. The family moved from aptly described Blow-the-Winds, on high ground outside St Ewe, to the cottage down the road even closer to Heligan, Plain-an-Gwarry. All three men appear routinely in the Labour Book throughout 1914. William, at 52, was by this time too old to go to war; Richard, the carpenter son, was 'pigeon-chested' and therefore deemed unfit. Only his brother Fred, the mason, succeeded in enlisting.

Fred Paynter joined the Royal Army Medical Corps and on 15th August 1915 was posted to the Balkans. At some point he transferred to the Royal Engineers and later to 16th Battalion, the Tank Corps. Ken told us that Fred got pneumonia and was withdrawn from service and sent to hospital. The following day the tank he had been serving in was blown up and all his comrades were killed. He eventually returned home in 1919. Ken and his wife Muriel brought not only his photo in uniform but also his three war medals to Heligan recently, where my colleagues and I were thrilled to examine them in the flesh and record them for posterity.

Survivor, Fred Paynter

Fred Paynter's medals include: The Inter-Allied Victory Medal issued in 1919, the 1914-1915 Star and the British War Medal

ROYAL FLYING CORPS AUXILIARY HOSPITAL,
HELIGAN,
PENTEWAN, R.S.O.
CORNWALL.

On 11th November 1918 Germany signed the Armistice with the Allies and the Great War was finally over. The Heligan Labour Books show that in the three years up to Summer 1917, the outdoor staff at Heligan reduced from 22 (sometimes 23) to 8; ie. down to only a third of full strength. We know that during the conflict at least six local families lost sons, brothers, fathers, husbands, lovers who had worked at Heligan sometime before the war. We have found no record of the outdoor labour force that remained here at the close of hostilities.

The "Mansion" had been given over to the Military as a convalescent hospital for wounded officers and Squire Jack had been living at Croan, twenty-odd miles away. There is no doubt he retained involvement at Heligan and one can only assume there was continuity of employment for the few remaining 'old retainers'. At a minimum, food and transportation was still required and some productive areas are known to have been utilised or set up closer to Heligan House.

Yet another of our gifts of fortune connected us with not one but two ladies in possession of wartime albums, recording the experiences of officers who took

Officers convalesce at Heligan on return from the Great War

"*Monkey Worship*"

"*Taylor hunting the Emu*"

respite in the tranquil, fading grandeur of Heligan. The beauty of the surroundings must have provided a haven indeed. The pictures here, from three separate sources (one noting "Drawing Room full of most gorgeous things"), certainly evoke treasured moments of gentle pleasure, friendship, kindness and fun, amid the tortured memories of past horrors.

Subsequently Jack Tremayne returned to Heligan; but it is reported that he could "no longer live with the ghosts", residing locally until he purchased Villa Boccanegra on the Mediterranean in 1923 and in due course settled there.

Frederick R. Draycott held the position of Head Gardener during the 1920s and early 30s and lived at the Steward's House, behind Heligan House. Sixty years later, in the early 1990s, his son Frederick E. Draycott drove himself down from the Wirral in a tiny Morris, to revisit the scene of his youth. He recalled the summer-long job of de-bugging the vines in the Paxton House and, at over eighty, was still able to visualise and put to paper the whole layout of the Mansion and surrounding buildings, with their uses – difficult enough if you have measuring tools for a site in front of you; but working out of his head alone, his hand-drawn plan *(reproduced overleaf)* is a phenomenal, vibrant recreation.

In 1929 Sydney and Muriel Williamson moved to Heligan. They were friends of the Tremaynes and had run a sheep station in New Zealand. They already had two grown-up children and were clearly very enthusiastic about the Gardens now in their care. Their connections with New Zealand enabled them to continue to

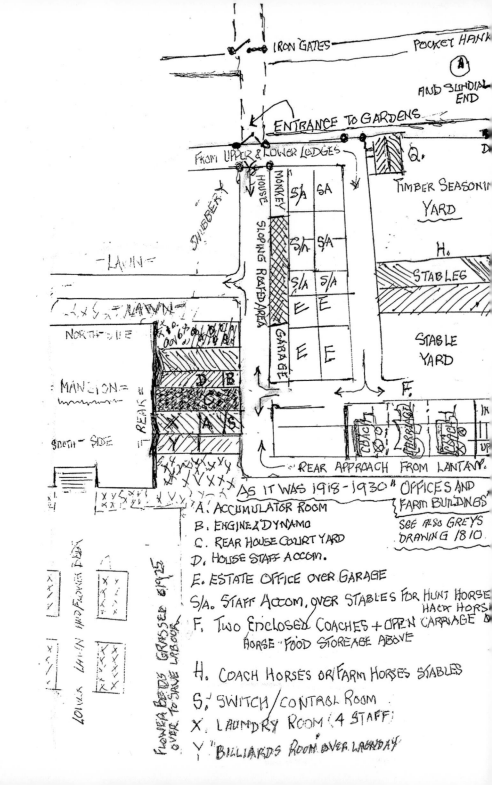

"AS IT WAS 1918–1930"

A. ACCUMULATOR ROOM
B. ENGINE & DYNAMO
C. REAR HOUSE COURT YARD
D. HOUSE STAFF ACCOM.
E. ESTATE OFFICE OVER GARAGE
S/A. STAFF ACCOM. OVER STABLES FOR HUNT HORSE HACK HORS
F. TWO ENCLOSED COACHES + OPEN CARRIAGE & HORSE FOOD STORAGE ABOVE
H. COACH HORSES OR FARM HORSES STABLES
S. SWITCH/CONTROL ROOM
X. LAUNDRY ROOM (4 STAFF)
Y "BILLIARDS ROOM" OVER LAUNDRY

"OFFICES AND FARM BUILDINGS"
SEE ALSO GREYS DRAWING 1810

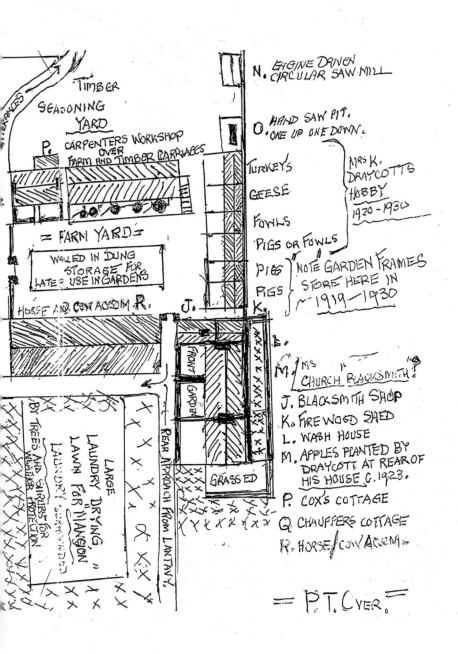

TIMBER

SEASONING
YARD

P. CARPENTERS WORKSHOP
OVER
FARM AND TIMBER CARRIAGES

= FARM YARD =

WALLED IN DUNG
STORAGE FOR
LATER USE IN GARDENS

HORSE AND COW ACCOM R.

J.

FRONT
GARDEN

REAR APPROACH FROM LANTAVY.

LARGE
LAUNDRY
DRYING,
"LAWN FOR MANSION
LAUNDRY" SUPERINTENDED
BY TREES AND SHRUBS FOR
WEATHER PROTECTION

GRASSED

N. ENGINE DRIVEN
CIRCULAR SAW MILL

O. HAND SAW PIT.
ONE UP ONE DOWN.

TURKEYS

GEESE

FOWLS

PIGS OR FOWLS

PIGS

PIGS

K.

Mrs K.
DRAYCOTTS
HOBBY
1920-1930

NOTE GARDEN FRAMES
STORE HERE IN
~ 1919 — 1930

M. Mrs
CHURCH BLACKSMITH

J. BLACKSMITH SHOP
K. FIREWOOD SHED
L. WASH HOUSE
M. APPLES PLANTED BY
DRAYCOTT AT REAR OF
HIS HOUSE C. 1923.

P. COX'S COTTAGE

Q. CHAUFFERS COTTAGE

R. HORSE / COW ACCOM.

= P.T.O. VER. =

Almost the final photo from Damaris Tremayne's album of Heligan, dated 1920

Jack purchased Villa Boccanegra, Bordighera, from the renowned horticulturist, Miss Ellen Willmott, a contemporary of Gertrude Jekyll. The villa, with its cliff-top Mediterranean garden, was sited not far from La Mortola, the Hanbury Garden near Ventimiglia, whose design also dated back to the late nineteenth century.

Heligan House and Gardens c. 1930

acquire plants from foreign climes. Mrs Williamson organised the running of the garden and worked in it herself. Photographs suggest that it is during their tenancy that the Jungle (the Tremayne's "Japanese Garden") must have been at its most sublime, carpeted with lilies and primulas *(below)*. In addition, Muriel Williamson was reputed to have been one of the most beautiful women ever seen and these few snapshots show she brought all the elegance and glamour of the period to Heligan.

Our picture of the thirties is built up from the personal recollections of then young people whose parents visited or worked there. Extraordinarily, for a few

years, there appear to have been more gardeners employed than before the Great War and the Home Farm was maintained; but these first-ever tenants at Heligan House did not carry the huge responsibilities for the maintenance of the woods and surrounding tenant farms. Surnames familiar from the old Labour Books reappear: Dyer, Brown, Baber, Pearce – whether they be the old generation or the new. Charity Rowlandson, who was a playmate of young Jimmy Williamson, recalled of Heligan, "I never remember seeing a bramble in the gardens and the numerous paths were in perfect order... It had a first-class reputation. When the Prince of Wales visited the Carlyon Bay Hotel with Mrs Simpson in the 1930s, he asked if they could come and see it, which they did." F. R. Draycott showed them around. There was an entourage of 8 inside staff and strict protocol for hospitality.

Muriel Williamson in flight suit, harvesting vegetables

It warms the cockles of the heart to find that William Paynter continues in employment at Heligan and that Fred had recently married and moved to St Austell, his son Ken (our window on this world) born in 1931.

For a while the emus continued in residence below the House and Flora's Green became an immaculate lawn again, hosting a round of smartly turned out church fêtes as ever. But with the advent of the Second World War everything gradually collapsed and by the early '40s the ageing Williamsons were gamely struggling almost on their own. Both Muriel and Sydney died in 1943. Jack Tremayne had left Italy in a hurry to return to Cornwall in 1939, but none of the Tremayne family ever lived in the Mansion again and it was subsequently tenanted out once more. Jack remained childless, so the inheritance passed down through the line of his older sister, Grace Damaris Matilda.

Several people have come forward with memories of having been evacuated to Heligan during the Second World War. They mostly stayed on tenant farms and some came to the Gardens *(left)*.

Heligan House was requisitioned and the American Army's 38th Engineer Regiment stayed between April and June 1944, practising landing on nearby Pentewan Beach in the run-up to D-Day. Mines were duly blown up on the Winnick and an impressive array of landing craft carried out exercises. Officers were billeted throughout the surrounding fields and woods owned by the Tremaynes. This build-up to the invasion only lasted about six weeks but £1,345. 4s. 2d. was thereafter paid for damages to the property. The hardcore that was rolled out onto Flora's Green remained in situ until 1991. Interestingly, Heligan was also used as a billet for five Italian prisoners-of-war, who had "emergency full-time employment" and their work was found to be "entirely satisfactory". We have several mentions of the Cornwall Service of Youth holding their Second International Summer Camp amongst the "tropical and sub-tropical plants and trees" in the grounds of Heligan in 1946, with at least one POW still present. Sir John, Jack's nephew visited with his wife, provided a tour of the Gardens and signed autographs. The Wishing Well was a favoured meeting spot and an old album bears evidence that much fun was had by all. There were also formal conference sessions, one illustrated here given by A. L. Rowse.

However, Jack Tremayne was by this time ailing and had settled at Rock Cottage in nearby Pentewan during the war with his Italian manservant. Ken Paynter recalls

International students attend a lecture by A. L. Rowse before a rendition of 'Chevaliers de la Table Ronde, allons voir si le vin est bon' under the rafters of the old Stable Block in 1946

visiting him there, with his father and uncle, almost in reciprocation for the call the old Squire had paid them after the death of his grandfather, William Paynter, in 1943. The steady history of the Paynter family over the decades had been interrupted by tragedy at this point. In December 1943 Minnie Paynter was nursing her father, William, who had developed pneumonia. She fell down stairs one night at Plain-an-Gwarry and broke her neck. William struggled to find help for her in the freezing weather; but they both died. There was a joint funeral at St Ewe.

Jack himself died in Italy in 1949, aged 80, during a visit back to Bordighera, and was driven home to join his ancestors. At his memorial service in St Ewe Church a benediction was pronounced by the Bishop of Truro, Dr. Joseph Hunkin, who was himself a prominent horticultural figure in Cornwall. There was subsequently a fire at Heligan House in which family records and possessions were lost and the remaining contents were auctioned. This moment seems to have sealed the fate of Heligan.

During the first years of restoration in the early 1990s, Tim and John Nelson had the honour of giving two separate special guests their own tours of the emerging gardens – momentous returns to Heligan for contrasting characters with their own connections. They wheeled the austere and by then famous poet

---

THE WEST BRITON – April 1949

SQUIRE OF HELIGAN
Memorial Service at St Ewe Church

The memorial service for the late Mr. John Tremayne, of Heligan, was largely attended at St. Ewe Church on Saturday. The Rector, the Rev. S. J. Rust, officiated, and the Bishop of Truro (Dr. J. W. Hunkin) pronounced the Benediction. The Rev. D. W. Holt (vicar of Mevagissey) was also present. The ashes were placed in the family vault. A large number of farmer tenants attended. Cornwall Constabulary was represented by Supt. H. Osborn (St. Austell), and St. Austell Urban Council by Mr. W. R. Nicholas (chairman).

Mr. A. L. Rowse, who was unable to be present at the service, has written the following tribute :-

John Tremayne was the last in the direct male line of the senior branch of the Tremaynes, one of the oldest Cornish families going back to the Middle Ages. In the sixteenth century the family provided an intimate and trusted servant of Queen Elizabeth's in Edmund Tremayne: it is said that he was racked at the time of the Courtenay conspiracy, in Mary's reign, in the hope of gaining evidence to implicate the Princess Elizabeth. On her accession he was rewarded: he became Clerk of the Privy Council. He had two famous brothers, Nicholas and Andrew, who were twins and inseparable ; in death they were not divided, both being killed in France, at Havre, in 1564.

The Heligan branch of the family has been settled in the parish of St. Ewe since Elizabeth's reign, when they were Catholic Recusants and as such suffered for their convictions. In the seventeenth century they were Royalists, providing a Governor of St. Mawes for the King, one who held out in Pendennis Castle to the last, and an eminent lawyer of the Restoration period who, as a young man, wrote home to Cornwall a vivid account of the Great Fire of London.

Something of these strains were to be seen in John Tremayne, who represented both branches of the family and was the head of the clan. Landowner of the old school, he had public spirit: he cared much for the look of the landscape, loved old buildings and knew a great deal about them, and in the 1914-1918 war he turned Heligan into a military hospital in which he worked. He had great distinction of bearing and the beautiful manners of an older and better world. A man of taste, with an instinct for beauty, he imprinted it on his surroundings, in the pictures and furniture he collected, in the gardens he created both in Cornwall and at the Villa Boccanegra where he died. It is sad to think that those wonderful gardens at Heligan, with the massed rhododendrons he loved now coming into bloom, will see him no more. And sadder still for his friends and those who loved him for they knew that along with that elusive sensitive spirit there went a loyal and generous heart.

and Elizabethan historian, A. L. Rowse, then in his twilight years, around the recovered Rides of the Northern Gardens and admired the view from the recently restored Northern Summerhouse, out across St Austell Bay. In 1925 "A. L." had become the youngest ever working class student to be elected a Fellow of All Soul's College, Oxford. He originated from a clay village north of St Austell. He now lived at Trenarren, a beautiful but isolated hamlet on Black Head, the dark headland which frames the opposite end of the bay at Pentewan. The newspaper report of Jack Tremayne's death *(opposite)* shows his respect for a gentleman whose ways were rooted in the past.

The other visitor was far from austere, or famous, but the delightful elderly lady, Mary Thomas. She was accompanied by her daughters Gill and Sue for what turned out to be her final visit to what had been her home up until some twenty or so years before. Commander and Mrs Thomas had become the new tenants of Heligan House in the 1950s, where Gill and Sue had lived as children. They brought a marvellous black and white photograph of their parents standing outside the old door into the Flower Garden, under the enormous *Camellia reticulata* 'Captain Rawes' (recorded in *The Gardeners' Chronicle* article of 1896), which smothered the wall. They also showed us an aerial view of Heligan House and surroundings in the 1950s. To the north-east the agricultural buildings remained in agricultural use, though far from immaculate; mown lawns are in evidence close to the other three sides of the house, including the Sundial Garden. Three separate glasshouses are still intact in the Flower Garden, but the Melon Yard is consumed by overgrowth and the glazing of the Melon House almost entirely collapsed.

Cmdr. Thomas had been a keen camellia grower, continuing the specific enthusiasm of at least three past squires. Some of Heligan's superb present-day collection is attributable to his own plantings. There is even a rare specimen on the Western Ride named after his wife, which we have successfully propagated. The Thomases geared their harvest towards commercial enterprise, sending cut flowers and foliage to Covent Garden. Camellias were the prime subject.

Jim Varcoe surveys his domain in the 1950s. The District Valuation of 1911 marks a new free-standing glasshouse in the Flower Garden and the 1914 workbooks mention a Carnation House – probably the structure on the right

(Princess Alexandra's wedding bouquet contained white camellias from Heligan.) They also grew snowdrops, violets, freesias, anemones and daffodils, as well as lavender and roses, for the same purpose. What a heaven for their daughters to grow up in, with fields and horses and adventures with friends, amid encroaching decay. The exterior of the house was consumed by the creeper. With very limited resources the challenge of maintenance became overwhelming and Cmdr. Thomas died in 1963.

Gill and Sue have become my good friends, but retain their family archive and their desire to record their own history of Heligan in the future. This includes the establishment of the Alpha-Omega Farm Training Scheme, recalled by a number of contacts but beyond the scope of this book. We have been privileged however to gain some further insights into the Gardens during this period, from Fred Varcoe and his wife, May, who were employed by the Thomases, and from the daughter of his namesake, Jim Varcoe. "They were not related", she insisted, and apparently did not get on, though they appear to have shared the responsibility for the entire garden as well as the infamous Drive.

Jim Varcoe was originally employed by Jack Tremayne in the 40s and lived with his family *(below)* at Lower Lodge. The Squire required him to have the whole length of the Drive hand-swept by 8am daily. Jim had responsibility for the productive areas, which included the Vegetable Garden; whereas Fred came in the '50s to look after the Pleasure Grounds and general maintenance, dusting the paths with sea-sand annually to keep the weeds at bay and harvesting camellias for market. Jim continued in service at Heligan under the Thomases, retiring in

1962. I took his daughter Kathleen on a tour of the Gardens and she identified those places she had known as a child – and those she had not. The chief route through the Northern Gardens up from Heligan House had been through Sikkim and up Western Ride. The Eastern Ride was not in use and she had never seen the Melon Yard. The Carnation House in the Flower Garden was extant within a sheltered area fully cropped by her father (though by 1990 it was derelict and consumed by bramble). The old rusting kettle we found in the Head Gardener's Office in 1990 had been her father's. Kathleen was moved to donate to us her Heligan memento, the white glazed tea mug she recalled him using when as a small child she had visited him there.

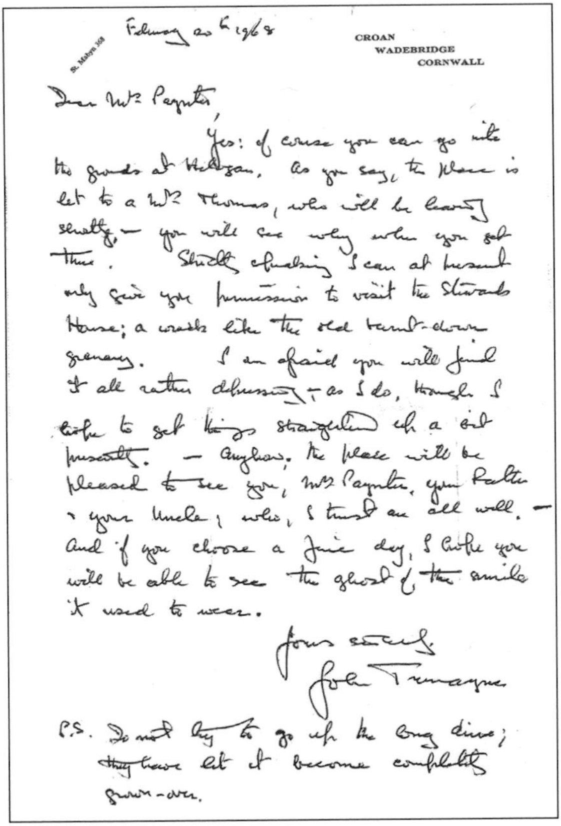

Handwritten letter:

February 26th 1968

CROAN
WADEBRIDGE
CORNWALL

Dear Mrs Paynter,

Yes: of course you can go into the grounds at Heligan. As you say, the place is let to a Mr Thomas, who will be leaving shortly — you will see why when you get there. "Strictly speaking" I can at present only give you permission to visit the Steward's House; a wreck like the old burnt-down granary. I am afraid you will find it all rather depressing — as I do, though I hope to get things straightened up a bit presently. — Anyhow, the place will be pleased to see you, Mrs Paynter, you & your Uncle; who, I trust are all well. — And if you choose a fine day, I hope you will be able to see the ghost of the smile it used to wear.

Yours sincerely,
John Tremayne.

P.S. Do not try to go up the long drive; they have let it become completely grown-over.

The day Kathleen got married in St Austell in 1963, she had returned to Heligan to visit the ailing Cmdr. Thomas. Thereafter the Gardens – and the Drive – slipped into almost complete obscurity.

In 1968 Ken Paynter asked Jack's nephew, Sir John Tremayne (*né* Babington), whether he could take his uncle and his father, Fred Paynter – both elderly now – back to visit Heligan. Sir John's reply is reproduced above. Shortly afterwards he made it known in horticultural circles that the Gardens were to be abandoned, and invited those interested to come and take cuttings from specimens of value.

On the death of his maternal uncle, Jack, in 1949, Sir John had inherited and retained this family property. His tenant Mrs Thomas stayed on for a while following her husband's death. After she and her daughters moved out, Sir John commenced a major project to refurbish and convert Heligan House to flats between 1971 and 1974. These were then sold on a 99-year lease. New residents included Ivor Herring, who redeveloped the Gardens immediately around the House and undertook research into the history of both, and Charity Rowlandson, who had played here with Jimmy Williamson in the 1930s.

What goes around, comes around.

Chapter Four NATURE'S EMBRACE

"You are too young to fall asleep for ever;
And when you sleep you remind me of the dead."

from *The Dug-out* by Siegfried Sassoon

In February 1990 John Willis (Tremayne descendant) ventured with Tim Smit into the totally overgrown and derelict Lost Gardens that were his inheritance; in retrospect almost a latter-day prince seeking to wake his Sleeping Beauty. Subsequently, it was Tim and John Nelson (local builder) who undertook the restoration on a shoe-string budget with a band of volunteers and the blessing of the Tremayne family.

These photographs were taken in 1991 by a friend of ours, Herbie Knott, a senior photo-journalist for *The Independent*, who was visiting us overnight from London... another gift of fate.

June 1991. I've arrived in Cornwall, late at night. Cornwall is wet and a gale is howling. My friend Tim Smit is waving his hands in the air: "You have to see this garden, mate, you have to see this garden."

The morning is calmer, but no "garden" in sight – just a dank mess of Cornish scrub. Tim appears, beaming: "Isn't this amazing? Follow me!" Captain Tim strides into a dripping rhododendron thicket, wellies oozing mud. He disappears. Deep silence… best to follow, emergencies 'n all.

Several thickets later there he is, standing by the Old Door to Heligan's walled garden. The weather has brightened. The door is ajar, a shaft of light shines through the crack. "Isn't this amazing, mate?" For the first time I agree, though not for reasons he imagined.

Beyond the door, strange creatures wandered through the undergrowth. Gnarled pensioners in shapeless garb moved in slow motion, hacking and slashing at immemorial brambles, whilst a demented priest dressed in sacrificial white swung an incense jar to mesmerise hidden sacred bees; this was a vision from *The Shining*. But the sight of the mythical bee boles, the finial of a submerged greenhouse here, a ruined cold-frame or two, and the wonderful wall with its door alongside the abandoned Head Gardener's Office convinced me this wasn't a bizarre film-set; but the site of a once-amazing garden, laid to sleep to dream.

Seventeen years on I'm astonished at the world-wide tribe of gardeners inspired by these Lost Gardens and by the Herculean effort it took to get Heligan up and running again. At the end of the day all you need to get going on a garden is one ray of hope, one little success, one shaft of light through the door, one rose that grows.

My own bible from the age of ten was *The Big Book of Gardening* by Charles Boff, first published in 1952. It featured line drawings of cheery pipe-smoking blokes wearing ties, digging in check shirts with sleeves neatly furled. All rather unlikely; but it taught me how to make a compost-heap, how to sterilise soil for seed-compost, how to build a cold-frame, how to make your own liquid manure, how to manage a garden – how to do things for yourself.

Seeing Heligan in 1991 brought all this back. More recently I've been privileged to put some of that theory into practice, since I moved to Hereford-shire. Heligan is a massive inspiration and it shows what can be done when you put your mind to it.

© *Herbie Knott; 2008   Herefordshire*

Postscript

In April 1992, less than a year after these scenes were recorded for posterity, by popular demand we opened "The Lost Gardens of Heligan" to the public. Ten years later, in 2002 alone, over 450,000 visitors streamed through the gates and Heligan was voted "The Nation's Favourite Garden" by *Gardeners' World* readers and viewers; a unique accolade bestowed to mark Alan Titchmarsh's departure from the enduring programme. What more could we ask, after all it had been through, than for Heligan to have captured the heart of the nation?

The Lost Gardens of Heligan are now open daily all year round and we offer hospitality to our guests as the Tremayne's would have done, using Heligan's own produce from the Gardens and estate in our own kitchens. We take a pride in our heritage as a focus for the good of the local community and hope that our forebears would approve of our ongoing endeavours in their name. At the time of writing there are 75 local people with permanent jobs here, of which 25 are 'outside staff', almost mirroring the situation at the outbreak of the Great War.

Tribute in deed.

The restored two-storey building nestles into the north-west corner of the Melon Yard, beside the old frames. In the dark, the door to the Thunderbox Room is almost invisible, but inside, the signatures remain – our memorial to the past

Postscript to Second Edition

Only 18 months after publishing this small booklet we already have the opportunity to update, add and amend for a reprint – thanks to its unexpectedly good reception, including the honour of receiving an *Holyer an Gof* Book Award in 2009 (winner in the category "Study of a Specific Locality") from Gorseth Kernow.

As we move on now to celebrate twenty years since the discovery of the Lost Gardens, public interest in the history of Heligan continues unabated, both from those with a possible historical connection and from our wider audience. Archiving and research is ongoing and fresh material continues to present itself.

For some years we have awaited with anticipation the publication of the 1911 Census, believing this to present our best chance of establishing the names of residents in the immediate run-up to the outbreak of the Great War. Somewhat comfortingly it consolidates existing anecdote, as well as opening up the opportunity for a whole new volume in the future.

J. Tremayne Esq is the registered occupier but not actually in residence at "Heligan Mansion" on April 2nd, 1911. His cousin Eric Arbuthurt is staying there, with seven indoor staff in attendance. R. W. Norman, whose letter of reference for Diggory Abbott is reproduced on page 36, is at "Heligan". This Robert William Norman is 43, a "domestic gardener", married with two young sons – no record of him being Head Gardener and there is no record of him in the Labour Books three years later (nor is it his hand that wrote them). He was born in Suffolk. Digory himself (officially spelt with one "G") is living at Heligan Mill and also

Those in residence at "Heligan Mansion" on the night of Sunday April 2nd 1911
© crown copyright image reproduced courtesy of The National Archives of England and Wales

recorded as a domestic gardener. He is 38 in 1911, not only married with two children but also, as we know, a desire for promotion. He was born in Tetcott, Devon, where his father was a gamekeeper.

There were several cottages at Heligan Mill and we find our friend and stalwart Archibald Smaldon also living there, with his wife Maud and three very young children, as well as James James (from the Heligan Estate Labour Book of August 1914), a "woodman" aged 48, married with a grown-up daughter. It was he who made that run for the emus. John Rowe (from the "Kitchen garden") is already a tenant at nearby Little Henna, so appears to have been employed as a gardener for at least 6 years – and probably right through the Great War.

Notable from this recently released National Archive is the fact that a minority of staff were born in the immediate locality, most originating from the South West region but some from as far away as the Home Counties, Scotland and even India.

*

Continuing to use the Heligan Estate Labour Books of 1914-17 as our richest source material, further cross referenced with the archive of the D.C.L.I. Regimental Museum, we may now have discovered (but cannot verify) what happened to three more of the recorded Heligan staff who had not yet arrived here in 1911:

H. Pascoe *(see page 38, recorded as cutting lawns and weeding in August 1914)* could have been Corporal H. Pascoe – D.C.L.I. 1st/4th Battalion, No. 200104 – died 22/11/1917 and buried in the Jerusalem War Cemetery, Israel.

W. Perry, according to the Labour Book, worked in the Heligan quarry. He could have been Private William G. Perry – D.C.L.I. 7th Battalion, No. 16660 – died 27/08/1918. Son of Mr and Mrs William Perry of Little Polgooth, south of St Austell, he was buried in the Berlin South Western Cemetery, which suggests he may have been a prisoner-of-war.

A. Rundle, also a quarryman, could have been Albert Rundle – D.C.L.I. No. 201292, a Corporal/Acting Quartermaster Sergeant – who was "mentioned in despatches" for bravery.

This brings the possible death toll amongst Heligan staff who enlisted up to eight, with possibly three survivors.

*

Last but certainly not least, members of the Tremayne Family also demonstrated exceptional bravery as well as suffering terrible losses at this time. All five of Jack Tremayne's nephews served in the Great War:

Sir John Tremayne (*né* Babington), John Willis's grandfather, was the long-lived hero of the Royal Flying Corps who inherited Heligan on Jack's death *(afore-mentioned on page 73)*, while two of his brothers were lost in this period. Hugh Babington, Lieutenant in the Royal Navy, was awarded the DSC and died in 1919, aged 27. Ralph Vivian Babington served in the Coldstream Guards and died aged 19 in 1917, just three weeks before Percy Carhart.

They both fought at Passchendaele and their memorials lie but three miles apart.

Candy Smit, April 2010

IN APPRECIATION

A cast of hundreds contributed to the care of Heligan House, Gardens and Estate during the past century – far too many to mention here within the focus of this small booklet. I have endeavoured to include and credit as many as possible, not to misrepresent anyone and to maintain contact wherever possible. Any errors or missing attributions will gladly be amended in future editions. Please forgive the sins of omission and feel free to continue to bring your archive and memories back to Heligan, so that they can form part of a more comprehensive archive held in our Library for posterity.

I would particularly like to thank friends and relatives of past players who have so willingly shared their memories and archive, with me as well as third parties, over the last decade and more. Some are themselves now deceased. There have been some emotional moments and we are friends in the knowledge that this publication only scratches the surface of Heligan History, leaving its soul intact.

Damaris Tremayne, Penelope, John and Antonia Willis – for Tremayne archive;
Margaret Fricker – for H. D. Wootton archive, pages 26-27 top;
Brian Rainsford, 15 bot; Colin Tyler, 24 top & bot; Trudi Pitts, 32, 33; Sylvia Davies, 34;
Dorothy Brookes, Aubrey Lane, 36; Nora Loxham; Ken Paynter, 35, 59 bot, 60 top, 70, 73;
Philip Guy, 46; Barbara Palmer, 48-49; Perren Dyer, 50; Hugh Warne, 52;
Lilian Currah and Carole Luscombe, 54;
Sarah Stokes, 61 bot, 62 top left & mid right, 63 top left and bot;
Sallie Penman, 62 bot, 63 top right; Peter Terrell, 62 top right;
Fred Draycott, 64-65; Ros Henry, 66 mid & bot left & right, 68 top; Anna Corns, 68 bot;
Tab White, front cover photo, 67 top & bot right; Charity Rowlandson; Peter Walters;
Kathleen Kendall, 71, 70; Fred and May Varcoe; Gill Bunker and Sue Williamson

This publication would never have materialised without the supporting research undertaken by:

Philip McMillan Browse, Frances Scholar, John Usmar, Stuart Fraser, Peter Lavis, Wendy Sharpless, Barry Yelland at The D.C.L.I. Regimental Museum, Kym Prout at Landscapes South West, Gordon Kane at Mevagissey Museum, David Holman and Ann Hicks of Cornwall Family History Society

Additional archive and pictures of monuments courtesy of:

The Trustees of the Imperial War Museum, London; R.H.S. Lindley Library, London;
North Devon County Record Office, Barnstaple (Heligan Estate Labour Books);
Cornwall County Record Office, Truro, and Cornish Studies Library, Redruth;
Geof Prettyman and Bob Evans, Pentewan Old Cornwall Society;
Commonwealth War Graves Commission, 47 top, 49 bot;
All Saints, St Ewe and St Goran Churches;
Cranston Fine Arts, 51 top left; Jim Porter, 51 top right;
The National Archives of England and Wales, 78

Photographs:

J. C .L. Tremayne and H. D. Wootton for almost all of Chapter One;
Herbie Knott, pages 2, 3, 4, 5, 6, 74, 75, 76, back cover;
David Hastilow, 8 top; Charles Francis, 7, 37, 38-39, 58 bot, 77;
Candy Smit, inside front cover, title page, 47 bot; Archie Smith, 49 mid left;
Lorna Tremayne, 49 medals; Peter Lavis, 51 bot left and right, 52 bot left & right, 53 bot left, 55 bot;
Mel Quested, 22, 53 top left and right; Jon Heslop, 55 top;
Julian Stephens, 59 top; Russell May, 60 bot;
Ruth Perkins, inside back cover

The Family Tree of the Tremaynes was drawn by Ruth Perkins; the map on p.56-57 comes from the French newspaper, *L'Illustration*, dated 19.12.1914; front cover design by Russell May